"I never knew what was driving m[...] *Danger Habit*! This book has help[...] speed can be used for good, rather than as a destructive force in my life."

—CHANDLER BROWNLEE
President, Christian Surfers United States

"When I was in my late twenties I volunteered to smuggle Bibles across the Chinese border. It was one of the most terrifying and thrilling adventures of my life. Up until that time I had done many things to experience the adrenaline rush that I craved. And like Mike, I never fully met that need until I gave that area of my life over to the purposes of Christ—then I discovered a life of true adventure that brought satisfaction and lasting purpose. I would dare anyone who feels driven to experience life to the fullest to read this book."

—TRI ROBINSON
Senior Pastor of the Vineyard in Boise, Idaho and author of
two books, *Saving God's Green Earth* and *Revolutionary Leadership*

"Through the honesty and transparency of his life and writing, Mike reinforces that crucial need for people who are relentlessly driven for new challenges and experiences to constantly seek and be vulnerable to God's movement in our lives."

—CHRISTIAN BUCKLEY
President, Covered Images

"*The Danger Habit* reads like an ops plan for God's very own 'special forces'...His warriors with extreme natures. Barrett puts them solidly in the fight...the Right fight. Anyone battling to understand how to combine thrill and theology, risk and reverence, will find this book an inspiring guide."

—LT. STEVE ELLIOTT
Wisconsin's 2001 Police Officer of the Year

The Danger Habit

mike barrett

Multnomah Publishers

THE DANGER HABIT

published by Multnomah Publishers

A division of Random House, Inc.

© 2006 by Mike Barrett

International Standard Book Number: 1-59052-740-2

Cover design by The DesignWorks Group, Inc.

Interior design and typeset by Katherine Lloyd, The DESK, Sisters, Oregon

Unless otherwise indicated, Scripture quotations are from:
The Holy Bible, New International Version © 1973, 1984 by International Bible Society,
used by permission of Zondervan Publishing House.

Other Scripture quotations are from:
The Holy Bible, New King James Version (NKJV) © 1984 by Thomas Nelson, Inc.
GOD'S WORD® (GOD'S WORD) © 1995 by God's Word to the Nations.
All rights reserved.
New American Standard Bible® (NASB) © 1960, 1977, 1995
by the Lockman Foundation. Used by permission.
The Bible in Basic English (BBE) © 1941, 1949
The Holy Bible, King James Version (KJV)
The American Standard Version (ASV) © 1901
Contemporary English Version (CEV) © 1995 by American Bible Society
The Amplified Bible (AMP) © 1965, 1987 by Zondervan Publishing House.
The Amplified New Testament © 1958, 1987 by the Lockman Foundation.
The Message by Eugene H. Peterson © 1993, 1994, 1995, 1996, 2000
Used by permission of NavPress Publishing Group. All rights reserved.

Multnomah is a trademark of Multnomah Publishers
and is registered in the U.S. Patent and Trademark Office.
The colophon is a trademark of Multnomah Publishers.

Printed in the United States of America

For information:
MULTNOMAH PUBLISHERS
12265 ORACLE BOULEVARD, SUITE 200
COLORADO SPRINGS, CO 80921

Library of Congress Cataloging-in-Publication Data
Barrett, Mike, 1963-
The danger habit / Mike Barrett.
    p. cm.
Includes bibliographical references.
ISBN 1-59052-740-2
1. Risk taking (Psychology)--Religious aspects--Christianity. 2. Christian life. I. Title.
BV4598.15.B37 2007
248.4--dc22   2006033371

07 08 09 10—10 9 8 7 6 5 4 3 2 1 0

To my beautiful wife Donna.
Your own love for risk appeared when you married me
ten weeks after we met. Ever since then you have been a
champion through the best and worst this adventure brings.

Table of Contents

Foreword

The author of this book, Mike Barrett, is self-admittedly of a "radical" temperament. You'll learn all about that in these pages. My own temperament is more what he terms "foundational"—but with some radical elements mixed in, some attraction to the edge and those who dwell out there. I may be foundational, but I've spent a good share of the past forty years interviewing and hanging with some very radical individuals—climbers, windsurfers, drug smugglers, big-water paddlers, deep-sea fishermen, lifestyle adventurers, and other wild-haired people, but mostly surfers.

Mike's subject here is the "danger habit," which is addictive behavior involving all sorts of edgework. The call of the wild and the lure of danger are powerful, and apparently answering them can kick off a spiral of adrenal intoxication leading to potentially unpleasant results. Surfers, for instance, have been steadily ratcheting up their adrenalin levels over recent decades as new techniques have opened the door to riding larger and larger waves. Last time I checked, waves over seventy feet tall have been successfully surfed with the assistance of personal watercraft (like Jet-Skis) and surfboards with footstraps.

Clearly any surfer who does that is crazy, but it's crazy-fun for spectators, who have their own connection to the danger habit. Meanwhile, the men and women who tow-surf into giant waves have become a new generation of Argonauts whose accomplishments are so beyond what was thought possible just a decade or so ago that they begin to exude the aura of human gods—what the Greeks called champions.

In this book, Mike explores the addictive (or habitual) nature of flirting with danger and pushing the envelope of inherent caution until life becomes a fearless (and maybe chemically altered) endeavor. His message is that addictive behavior of any sort (even addiction to a religion or its concomitant "divine comfort") is potentially problematic for the individual and at times for society as well.

George Gurdjieff, an early twentieth-century teacher of "esoteric Christianity," defined sin as "that which is unnecessary." By that standard, a lot of what we call "lifestyle" or action sports is sinful…an indulgence. And yet it's such great fun—thrilling for participant and voyeur alike!

To make a giant leap here: Although I don't have a "belief" system per se, it seems readily apparent to me that a Christian is someone who tries to do what Christ would have done in a particular moment or situation. Christ is the guy who was quoted as saying, "No slave can serve two masters, for a slave will either hate one and love the other, or be devoted to one and despise the other. You cannot serve God and wealth." But how about God and adrenaline?

Exposure to the wild and to danger develops strengths and understanding of principles that an individual can apply to other arenas. For instance, surfers are uniquely equipped to offer assistance in certain situations (like tsunamis, hurricanes, and other natural disasters). Surfers and other extreme-sports athletes are intimately aware of the quality of the environment and especially acquainted with machinations of nature. To take the experiences of danger and the lessons that came from them and apply a new understanding to the realities of our modern world is the greater labor of champions.

I believe that the transformation of the self-absorbed "danger habit" into heroic efforts for the common good represents one of the great possibilities for near-term positive evolution in human culture. Mike's revolutionary book could well be the first ripple in a new wave of consciousness that will lift the individual and mankind towards a more conscious and balanced future.

—Drew Kampion
Author of *The Way of the Surfer*
and editor of *The Surfer's Path*
October 2006

The Way You're Wired

People who like to play on the edge create their own language. Have you noticed? *Catching deep thick barrels. An off-the-wall. First ascent. Pulling a 900. E-ticket rides. Big air. Aced a 5.14a. Class 5 rapid. Diamond runs.* Talk like that means something to us. We're surfers, skaters, boardheads, kayakers, climbers, bikers, kiters, and serial entrepreneurs. As a group, we tend to feel most alive when we are living on the radical edge of things. We are constantly looking for adventure.

We have been called radical, extreme, hard charging, adrenaline junkies, and thrill seekers. Also freaks, lunatics, idiots, and worse. Whatever. We live outside the boxes handed to us by religion and culture, and we like it that way.

But it comes with a cost.

The same guy who's always grabbing a board and running out the door is likely to be running up a record of dumb choices in other areas of his life. The same guy who burns through jobs is probably also burning through relationships. Sooner or later we find we can't move fast enough to outrun the damage. And when it catches up with us, it hurts—bad.

My favorite quote from the last twenty years is by the boxer Mike Tyson. Iron Mike was meeting with reporters before a big title fight—against Buster Douglas in Las Vegas, I think. One reporter prefaced his question with something like this: "Mike, your opponent has been watching films of your other fights, training hard. He has a plan to beat you. What are you going to do about that?"

In his signature high-pitched voice and lisp, Mike Tyson said, "Man, everyone's got a plan...until they get hit."

I think about how many game plans Iron Mike changed with his thundering right. Fifty wins in his heavyweight career, to be exact—forty-four by knockout.

But I also think about all the hits I have given and taken, and how they've changed my plans too. A lot. For people like me—a little narcissistic, a little ADD, a lot risk junky—change seems to come only after a big hit. But is that all we can look forward to in our futures—taking one Tyson-like right hook after another to the temple of our selfish lives? I don't think so. This book is about another way to see ourselves, and a better way to change.

I am forty-two years old, and I cannot sit still in a meeting. I know that we're born with certain tendencies, traits, and dispositions that we carry throughout life. But I am changing, mostly as a by-product of the difficult journey I am on and the unwavering commitment God has made to keep hammering on me. And hammer me He does, faithfully, sometimes to the point where I feel I might not be able to take it anymore. It may be the same for you.

My friend and mentor, Vic Anfuso, once told me something that has rung true in my life. "If you read something you will gain knowledge. If you do not read the fine print, however, you will gain experience." That is the point of this book. To share the experiences I, and others throughout history, have endured as a result of not reading the fine print. We lived a good part of our lives feeding our danger habit and, as a result, jumped into the battle without an ax.

If you're beginning to recognize yourself in these words, then this book is for you. It's a book for people who like to burn the candle at both ends. It is for the trashed, crashed, and thrashed. It is for people who live for risk, and love it so much they'll risk another big hit almost every time.

But *The Danger Habit* invites you to explore the possibilities that God not only intentionally wired you for an extreme life, but He also has a healthy, promising way for you to make the most of what He created you to be.

Chapter 1

The Danger Habit

*My heroes are the ones who survived doing it wrong,
who made mistakes, but recovered from them.*

BONO

*A strong man knows how to use his strength,
but a person with knowledge is even more powerful.*

PROVERBS 24:5, GOD'S WORD

*As a kid, I always colored outside the lines and was
chided for not staying within them. In reality, it was
harder to stay inside. Outside was freedom of self and
expression of who God created me to be.*

TED GILLETTE, SURFER, BUSINESSMAN, PASTOR

More than an athletic exercise, surfing is an almost spiritual interaction with the forces of nature—forces that sometimes get the best of us. Which is what happened one Sunday afternoon when I went surfing in front of our home on the Oregon Coast with my fifteen-year-old son, Joel.

It was late January and, completely out of character, the sun was out in full force. A slight offshore wind lifted spray off the top edge of each wave. Two separate tow-surfing teams were at work in the water that day. I had done tow-surfing a few times and quickly realized that paying for the gas and breathing in the exhaust was not my cup of tea. However, walking across the street to surf with my son, unassisted by machinery, was pure and right.

Joel and I paddled out to the swells on the outside sand-bar. The eight-foot waves created a wave face of well over twelve feet. In surfing we call that "double overhead." And it was all of that and a bit more.

Looking things over, Joel decided he was out of his league and sat on his board just outside the impact zone while I tried to paddle into a few. Joel is on the high school swim team and a solid waterman for his age, but he has only been surfing for a few years, so he was intimidated on this day for good reason. I've been surfing on and off since I was ten years old, and I was pretty excited.

I caught my first wave, a moderate-sized one that hurled me down the line. I made a quick exit out the top of the wave as it began to close off into a thundering shore break.

As I paddled back out, Joel paddled for his first wave, a smaller swell that looked safer than the others we'd been see-ing. Joel is sensible. I respect him for that. For many reasons surfing with him and talking with him are deep and meaningful. Nearly twelve years ago Joel lost his mother, my first wife, to cancer. He was only five years old then and his younger brother Joshua was only two. Since then we have been close. Surfing together is a treasure I don't take lightly.

On this one beautiful Sunday, things suddenly changed for the worse. Much larger swells loomed on the horizon, what we sometimes call a "clean up set." Waves come in sporadic sets and at some surf spots the sets can build up in size over time. They're called "clean up sets" because they tend to clean up everything in their path—surfers, kelp, seals, logs…everything.

Joel began paddling as hard as he could toward shore. I paddled as hard as I could toward Hawaii. When a wave broke right in front of me, I ditched my board and swam as deep as I could. I felt my leash break and knew that my board was headed toward the beach. I was in for a fifteen-minute swim.

By this time, Joel was twenty yards closer to shore. I saw him get pummeled. The white water alone must have been eight feet high as it reached him. Later, he said it briefly pinned him to the bottom.

Surfers learn to take their time in these situations. Panicking or swimming too hard just depletes the oxygen in your blood and can hasten dehydration. That will bring on dizziness and fatigue, which increase your risk of drowning. So you just learn to relax and swim.

Which is what I did.

At one point during my long swim to the shore, I noticed

a Coast Guard helicopter flying over my head. I thought, *How convenient. If I were in trouble here, that guy would rescue me.* Cool! By the time I reached shallow water, I noticed a police officer walking down the beach toward my son, who was waiting near my board. Then I saw the local fire department backing their rescue jet skis toward the water while an ambulance crew unloaded equipment.

Who were they here to rescue?

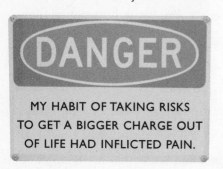

MY HABIT OF TAKING RISKS TO GET A BIGGER CHARGE OUT OF LIFE HAD INFLICTED PAIN.

I came out of the water down the beach from where my son and half a dozen others were standing. As soon as he spotted me, Joel looked immensely relieved. In minutes I learned that everyone was there to rescue me. Joel had seen my board come in without me, and I was in the water too far outside the huge swells to be visible. Thinking I was in trouble, he'd called 911.

The whole experience was embarrassing for me, but for Joel it was excruciating and nearly heartbreaking. Afterward, I made sure he knew that calling 911 had been the right thing to do. I was proud of him.

Later, the more I thought about it, the more my embarrassment turned to self-doubt. My habit of taking risks to get a bigger charge out of life had inflicted direct, unnecessary pain on my son.

What kind of father does that?

If you're like me, you can look in your past and find clues.

Built to Thrash

Living on the edge makes life more exciting, especially for people who need to escape. And as a kid, I really needed to escape some things. My heart must have been broken about five hundred times before I turned ten. Not that I'm alone in feeling that way, but those early school years were filled with experiences that made me question my worth. My memory is foggy now about much of it, but I remember mockery, meanness, getting beat up on the playground, being the last one picked for dodgeball. I remember lunches of a peanut-butter-and-jelly tortilla because we didn't have money for bread that week.

Things got better when I stumbled into skateboarding and surfing. My father bought me a ten-foot surfboard that I couldn't even carry to the water by myself. We lived across the street from the beach in Oxnard, California, and my parents could always find where I was surfing by looking for the line in the sand created by the tail of the forty-five-pound board I was dragging across the beach. There were summer days so hot I would do my best to run across the sand that burned my bare feet, periodically stopping to lay the board down and bury my feet deeper in the cooler part of the sand. Then I would gather the courage to make another one-hundred-foot run toward the water. The lifestyle fit me like a glove.

I also became one of the first-generation skateboarders. Without realizing it, my friends and I were on the bleeding edge of extreme sports before anyone was even using the term extreme sports. This was in the early seventies when California beach houses sold for $40,000, and Volkswagens and Datsuns were outselling American cars. We used to listen to scratched Beach Boys records on the turntable, or we got caught up in the great Los Angeles rock-radio wars between KMET and KLOS. Those were the days when we wondered if the Soviets were really going to bomb us, and President Nixon was telling us he was not a crook.

It's hard to believe now, but my first skateboard had metal wheels fit over a metal axle with no flex at all under the board. The ungodly noise it threw off echoed between houses down Ocean Drive, letting the whole neighborhood know that the skateboarders were out. Riding the asphalt streets on metal was enough to make your teeth fillings fall out. But we loved it. Escaping from the house to ride down the street with a few long-haired friends was pure joy and freedom. I remember riding on summer nights, turning so hard on concrete that our metal wheels would throw sparks from under the board.

Clay wheels improved things, but we still had to pack grease into the ball bearings to keep them from sparking, arcing, melting down, and seizing up. All the kids on my street got pretty excited when better technology finally came to the skateboard world in the form of polyurethane Simms wheels. Heck, I listened enough to my chemistry teacher to know that poly-anything meant the new wheels were going to be really cool. Those Simms wheels opened up a whole new world of going fast and turning hard. Ramp skating took off. Covertly draining the swimming pool at an empty house became the thing to do. Skate parks opened and skateboard magazines hit the shelves of surf shops and drugstores everywhere.

One day things changed for me. It was still in the pre-poly era. A few friends and I decided to take a trip to "the Cross" in Ventura. The wooden cross stood atop a manzanita-and-grass-covered hill with a three-mile road that wound its way down the hill from the cross on top to the town below. Back then, there were few homes on the way down. We thought it would be fun to ride our boards the whole way, pumping the tail hard to generate more speed, or weaving back and forth with long turns to slow ourselves down. We wanted to see who could make it to the bottom in one piece.

That was the beginning of a high-risk tradition. We'd spend summer evenings bumming rides to the top, then flying down the long descent, taking our chances. Everything would go just fine until one of us hit a rock. In those days, hitting even a small rock meant your body got launched into the air while your board stayed with the rock. What followed was a lot of tumbling, crunching, and sliding across the asphalt until you came to a bloody rest in the weeds beside the road. Every time we came around a corner and saw a cloud of red Ventura dust ahead, we knew someone had gone over the side or slid off into the bushes. I remember coming home with bloody arms, knees, elbows, hands, and a banged up chin. Except for the big smile on my face, my mother might have thought I had been in a car crash or a bad fight. I loved every minute of it.

I think that is when the danger habit actually started for me. You find something exciting, something you're good at (that has a high probability of disaster), and you go for it, all the while thinking you're the one kid on the street who can pull it off. I had found a way to make life interesting, to forget about the pain and the bad stuff going on around me. All I had to do was push myself past the limits others set for themselves. Plus, I had found the perfect sport—my parents didn't understand it and all the cool kids did it. Perfect. Living like that became my fix.

My choices had roots in my temperament. I've always been described by friends and family as high-energy or ADD. From the time I was in grade school, teachers tried to get my mother to put me on Ritalin, without success. Teachers typically described me as someone who "demonstrates risky behavior." One person called me an "unbridled horse," which I took as a compliment.

As with almost everything, people find their own versions of risky behavior. For example, I do not drive a jacked-up Hummer or base jump off antennas. Some do. I don't hele-ski or climb into cages for ultimate full-contact fighting. Maybe you do that. But I am certainly an extreme person by nature. And unfortunately, the personality dropped into this body by my Creator has caused me and others in my life varying amounts of grief. It is no surprise that extreme people tend to generate a lot of collateral damage. We experience a higher percentage of damaged relationships, ruined families, disappointed bosses, unhappy spouses, and financial trouble than others around us.

And where's the thrill in that?

A number of years ago, after struggling endlessly over what direction I should pursue in my life, I went to see a doctor. That visit turned into weeks of tests and interviews with a psychologist and my family doctor. Most of the tests I was given were easy, and the initial feeling I had was that I would sail past all this with the medical proof that I was fine and everyone else around me was screwed up. I would even have a doctor's note to prove it. But I was not so lucky.

The wrench in my plan came near the end of the psychological evaluation period (at somewhere around $200 an hour) when one of the tests they gave me had a time limit. As I approached the last third of the questions and the clock was approaching the time limit, I began to get frustrated and make mistakes. Then I became angry. *The test is designed wrong and this doctor is stupid!* I thought. The more frustrated I got, the more mistakes I made.

In the end I was diagnosed with ADHD, Impulsivity Type. (At the time, it felt more like ADHD, "I want to rip your head off" Type.) While I am reasonably smart and normal when things are calm, under pressure my mental capacity slides to about that of a sixth grader! Oh $#@%!

Though I'm thankful for God's guiding and healing hand
in my life, once a radical, always a radical. And my danger
habit still gets me in trouble. But I'm far enough down the
road that it's time to share my life message of honesty, hope,
and challenge with my fellow risk addicts.

Life on the Edge

Have you recognized some of your own instincts and passions, and maybe some of your own experiences, in my story?
If so, then you may have your own danger habit. I'm sharing my story so that others like me can avoid some of the
pitfalls we tend to fall into, and for a larger reason too—so
that you and I can reclaim the truth that we are loved by
God and created for a unique and important destiny.

But maybe you would say, "Inside I'm an extreme person,
but I guess I've mostly opted out. Look at me from the outside, and I'd look as normal as the next guy."

I'm sharing my story for you too. I've made similar choices
at times in my life, as you'll see in the pages ahead. Millions of
radicals are locked up in careers with annual pay raises, trying
to stay ahead of the mortgage payment, trying to do the
responsible, "mature" thing. Sometimes that's absolutely the
best thing to do. Problem is, you never change how you feel
inside. Deep down, you know you're wired for danger. And
you feel your vulnerabilities. You hope you don't ruin everything by running away with some mysterious lover with a

tattoo on her lower back, or joining a metal band, or setting off alone around the world.

The promise of what God can do with extreme people is huge, as I will try to show you in the chapters to come. But conversely, the threat to ourselves and others if we don't reclaim our lives for higher purposes is also huge—and tragic.

Living and working as I do inside the Oregon surfing community, I meet a lot of people who burn the candle at both ends. They always look for the edge, then jump over. Again and again, I see that the desire to push the envelope when we're young often progresses into destructive attitudes and behaviors when we are older.

It only makes sense. We extreme people love flying high above the skate-park bowl and flying "high" after smoking a bowl. Age and greater responsibilities don't necessarily change that. They just intensify and spread around the negative consequences.

I see people in my community who love extreme living yet have no clue why they love stuff that brings so much pain to them and others. (Truth is, they often seem to enjoy seeing themselves or others getting hurt because it takes the sting out of their own inner pain.) But pushing to get higher, crashing at a higher rate of speed, and living harder only makes sense in the darkness. It might still bring a thrill, but you just can't build a life on it.

In the pages of this book, I desperately want you to see

yourself in new ways. We seekers of the "Wow" have reason to feel refreshed, not like freaks or rejects. Every radical adventure junkie who would rather skydive than go to church has been created by God to take, or at least long for, a different path. Maybe He created us to blow through the harder rock of life and make new roads where others won't or

GOD NEEDS SOME OF US
TO BE CHANGE MAKERS,
NOT ROUTINE SUSTAINERS.

can't. You and I can't do extraordinary things (we can't even want to) without a measure of reckless passion for life, a disdain for the routine, and a thirst for some danger.

And God needs some of us to be change makers, not routine sustainers, to live dangerously, not just enjoy reading about it, to pioneer new ways of thinking and living because the old ways are tired and boring.

This isn't just a flakey spiritual idea, by the way. It's biology.

The Radical Gene

As it turns out, research suggests that a radical gene exists in the DNA of some people. Dr. Marvin Zuckerman of the University of Delaware found that some people are prone to be addicted to the natural chemicals released in the brains of people who take extreme risks, overcome fear, or take chances that "normal" people would not take. Calling it the "sensation-seeking personality," Zuckerman was able to create a scale of measurement to assess the underlying motivations of action-sports enthusiasts. Skydivers, extreme kayakers, and rock climbers tested among the highest on his scale.

In a 1994 issue of *Psychology Today*, Zuckerman reported on his research.[1] His conclusions in that article have special bearing on the purpose of this book. He says some studies are showing that a desire for risk may be innate in some people. It's not that we have a "death wish." Instead, risk works like a drug, triggering the parts of our brain that react to pleasure, so that taking chances becomes an addiction.

So, if we're physically engineered by God to take high risks and they can become an addiction to us, the stakes must be a lot higher than we could have imagined.

Let me get at this puzzling possibility by starting from the addiction end of Zuckerman's finding and pose a question: If God created us to crave behaviors that can invite addiction, damage, and even death, what important achievements that require the same temperament could He have in mind for us?

After giving it a lot of thought, here's where I've come down on that question: I believe that adventure, danger, and even the tendency toward addiction are uniquely connected to the real meaning of living by faith. In other words, radical people might be on to something—or very close without knowing it—that is at the core of real, radical Christianity.

I'm not saying that radical people are more important than every other kind of person. Not long ago, a close friend of mine told me, "Just because you are louder doesn't mean God will use you more." She's right. God doesn't prefer loudmouths to introverts. He deeply loves and pursues all kinds of people.

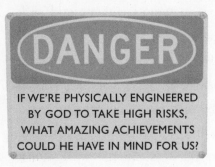

IF WE'RE PHYSICALLY ENGINEERED BY GOD TO TAKE HIGH RISKS, WHAT AMAZING ACHIEVEMENTS COULD HE HAVE IN MIND FOR US?

But still, if you and I are not mistakes who need to be neutralized and locked away, what could we possibly have to contribute to such a nonphysical, abstract, and "religious" topic as faith?

Let me try to explain.

The Faith-Risk Connection

One of the fathers of the Vineyard worship and church movement, John Wimber, used to say that faith was spelled "R-I-S-K." He believed true faith requires risk, and *risk-taking* can be an adventure. Even the most intelligent atheist or agnostic admits to their own dependence on the principles of "faith" when they embark on a new business venture or serious athletic accomplishment, whether it's taking an eco-challenge or climbing Mount Everest. This is because they have to work through so many unknowns, calculating risks, and deciding to make their move without really knowing where it will land them. In a sense, this is also faith.

Following Jesus actually requires a full dose of risk-taking or it will quickly become deadening religion, not the new life He came to give. The Bible description for pursuing a healthy danger habit is "living by faith" (Romans 1:17).

Anytime I see a person move deeper into a Christian form of faith, I can almost see on their face how risky it is for them. The spiritual blinders they wore (previously blocking out the eternal love God has for their soul) are removed, and they begin to step slowly into a world they have been suspicious of, and critical of, for so long. Talk about risk! What if they are wrong? What if nobody really has the answers, and what if the Bible is just a tribal book after all, only for Jews and early Christians? What if their family and friends think they are crazy or brainwashed? But, even more threatening than all this, what if their choice to live by faith in Him actually brings them into the vicinity of a very real and powerful God, One who has an unyielding desire to completely and miraculously change their life?

Adrenaline junkies have this godly attribute running amok in their lives without realizing that God has created them for a much greater, even eternal, purpose. Statements like these might rattle you at first because you're like so many risk takers who are congenitally suspicious of religion, church, and hype of all kinds. If so, I hope you'll open your mind to another way of viewing your life.

Recently I watched a show on FUEL TV about BASE jumpers—people who skydive from towers, monoliths, and bridges. They must have interviewed five or six guys who shared the joys of propelling their bodies at 150 miles per hour toward the ground nine hundred feet below.

As I watched them talk to the camera, I was struck by the fact that these same individuals could be changing the world if they would only align their addiction to danger with an

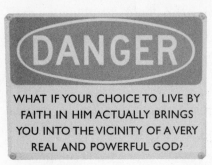

WHAT IF YOUR CHOICE TO LIVE BY FAITH IN HIM ACTUALLY BRINGS YOU INTO THE VICINITY OF A VERY REAL AND POWERFUL GOD?

authentic faith. Instead, they might as well be any small group of friends at any skate park or BMX track near you. They represent a subculture of hard-charging postmodern adventure seekers who live for themselves without apology.

You have to love their honesty, though. Most of the young people I know who avoid religion and love the adrenaline cultures are also painfully honest about themselves. They readily admit they are screwed up, and they can easily share their deepest heartaches and desires with each other. (And isn't that something the church is missing?) Yet my friends from that world are living with the consequences of being disconnected from their Creator and the Lover of their soul. In the end, I see many left holding binding addictions, empty friendships, empty bank accounts, and empty spiritual lives.

That's what can happen when an adventurer doesn't make the faith-risk connection, never finds a higher purpose (than selfish thrills) for the amazing way God made them, never signs up for the biggest thrill of all—a full-on, radical pursuit of God's best.

At Play with the Father

Some time ago I was staying in Hawaii with my family for the Christian Surfers National Leadership Conference. While there, my then six-year-old son, Caleb, started surfing with me. After months of planning the trip and talking to Caleb about how to surf, and how warm the water is in Hawaii, and how "cool" surfers are in Hawaii, we rented a long board off the beach in Waikiki and walked into the water.

We started by lying together on the deck of a ten-foot-long board and paddling out the one hundred yards to find waves among the hundreds of other pasty white tourists. On the way out, Caleb had some questions: What if I fall? What if we can't catch a wave? But once we were in position, he was ready. We slowly turned the board around and waited.

When a wave came, I started paddling as hard as I could while Caleb got ready to stand up in front of me and surf. He caught on pretty fast. Sometimes he would jump up before we even caught the wave. But when his timing was right, and the wave propelled us toward shore, you could have created cake frosting with the joy that poured out of Caleb's body. It was the most wonderful experience.

Oh, I forgot to mention that Caleb can't swim. I suppose that is what made my wife a bit nervous. Of course, to me,

the high stakes were somehow part of what made the experience so thrilling for both of us. (Note: The water was
crystal clear and about four feet deep, so if Caleb had slipped
off the board, I could have easily grabbed him and lifted him
to safety. This was not a Michael Jackson-dangling-his-son-
over-the-balcony scene.)

I tell this story because that day became a turning point
for Caleb. He had ventured into a place of danger with his
loving and protective father and emerged from the water alive
and changed. From that day on, he has called himself a surfer.

High-stakes adventure with the protection of a loving
father—that was the E-Ticket Ride for Caleb that day, and
the one for you and me in our pursuit of a meaningful life.
Make no mistake, the stakes for us are also high. The
notion of leaving behind what the "world" expects of us is
one thing, but the business of bearing our own soul to our
Creator is another, and one does not really know where it
leads. We wonder, What if it leads to my early death?
What if God calls me to poverty or a prison ministry?
What if I am tortured on the mission field? What if I never
get married? Hmmm.

For my son Caleb the questions, I think, were similar: What
if my dad paddles for a wave too big for me? What if he just rolls
off the back of the surfboard and lets me fall and drown?

As a loving father who intimately knows the sport of surfing, I would never let Caleb go. I would never let him drown.
I would never take a wave too big for him. But I would also

never—get this—in a million trillion years let him just sit on the beach in perfect safety.

I love him too much.

He's my dear child. He's not made for that kind of life. He's been specifically created for so much more, and he's been gifted with a passion to pursue.

So it is with you and me as we travel through this gift of life with our heavenly Father.

Some of us are made to be adventurers, artists, wanderers, hard-charging extreme people, and we've known it from our earliest years. Adventure is in our spiritual DNA. But God made us that way for a reason. From the time of our first breath, God wanted us to be charged up with passion for the life He gave us.

As you and I go forward in our journey of understanding, healing, and growth in this life of faith, God travels with us. He won't let us spiral into

I WOULD NEVER LET HIM JUST SIT ON THE BEACH IN PERFECT SAFETY.

oblivion. On the other hand, He won't let us just waste away on the beach either.

The ride up ahead is too promising for that.

A Profile of Opposites

I tend to be more radical and my wife is more foundational. I think that there is something about that, that draws me to her and vice versa—a desire for attributes that don't come naturally to us. But our differences can be a big source of conflict as well.

SPENSER REYNOLDS, SURF ARTIST, HUSBAND

No man in the world has more courage than the man who can stop after eating one peanut.

CHANNING POLLOCK, AMERICAN PLAYWRIGHT, CRITIC, AND SCREENWRITER

In Oregon the ocean is always cold. In winter, water temperatures hover in the forties and fifties. That's freezing compared to waters most surfers frequent. Without a wetsuit, you have maybe eight minutes before you pass out from hypothermia.

On top of the cold-water issue is the Great White Shark

issue. Just in my little beach town of Lincoln City, I know two surfers who have been attacked by Great Whites in the last few years. One friend spent time in the hospital nursing a large bite out of his left leg. The other narrowly missed getting chomped by sliding to the front his board just as the shark was biting down on the tail. But the fact is, the harsh surfing conditions in Oregon are great news for those of us who don't care about the cold and choose to believe we won't taste good to the average shark—because there's one thing worse than either cold water or sharks, and that is a crowd.

We don't like crowds! It might sound crazy, but whenever I surf in California or Hawaii, I always return home to my cold water and Great White Sharks with a sense of relief. I'm home, where I get to take more waves with less hassle. I love the times when I'm out there with one or two friends, surfing until we're too tired to stand up, relishing every minute of our time in God's creative expression of liquid wonder. Finding our place in His expansive ocean is a spiritual experience.

I've surfed the waves so much in my life that they have become the best metaphor I know for radical and foundational personalities. We're going to look at both of these personality types in this chapter, and see why.

Waves are a combination of two primary forces in nature—wind and tides. The best waves to surf are created when winds from a faraway storm collaborate with an incoming tide. This partnership of wind and tide has worked together since the beginning of creation, inviting even the animals to surf along the swell lines of the sea. It's common to see seals swimming with the waves near shore, or pelicans gliding just inches above the building swells, pulling out only moments before the wave crests near the beach. To a surfer, this is clear and compelling proof that God made waves for surfing.

The two forces have different personalities. Since tides are driven by the rotation of the earth and the gravitational pull of

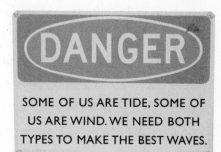

DANGER

SOME OF US ARE TIDE, SOME OF US ARE WIND. WE NEED BOTH TYPES TO MAKE THE BEST WAVES.

the moon—both of which are unchanging—tides are predictable and dependable. You can chart them years in advance.

"Predictable and dependable"—those words describe the tides, but they can also describe certain types of people that I call "foundational." They're the reliable, ordered, responsible ones in this world.

Wind, on the other hand, is neither predictable nor dependable. Wind can be tracked and measured as it moves with a storm or approaches a coastline, but no one can predict winds months or years in advance. In their own way, winds have as much power as tides, but they express that power in different ways.

My word for wind is "radical." In the same way that some people are foundational, others are radical. By that I mean they are difficult to control, changeable, and—compared to tides—not very dependable. At the risk of sounding like a Native American shaman, I am more like wind.

What is true for waves also seems true for people. Some of us are tide—dependable, predictable, and strong. Some of us are wind—more surprising, more changeable, and potentially strong in an entirely different way. We need both types to make the best waves—and the best lives.

I have four kids, and my wife and I knew from very early in their lives which ones were radical and which were foundational. Take Caleb. At seven, he is remarkably patient and insightful for his age. In fact, he has the courage and discipline referenced in the Channing quote at the beginning of this chapter. He is the kid who could keep from eating a cookie today if that would allow him to eat two cookies tomorrow. I still can't do that. Even though he loves to do risky things, like surfing with his dad, he is as foundational as they come.

On the other hand, there is Ellie. At five, she would not only eat today's cookie but then fearlessly try to charm or manipulate me into letting her eat all the other cookies too. She is what I call radical.

I realize that any broad generalization has its limits. In fact, what I am describing may not apply to you at all. So let me qualify this.

First, I'm not using these two labels in some clinical sense—like "ADHD, Impulsivity Type"—but simply as helpful descriptions. I'm not trying to compete with Jung's eight personality sets, or the sixteen temperament types of Myers-

Briggs. What we need for this book is something simpler that still rings true from everyday experience.

Second, I admit that all the people in this world are not easily or accurately placed into just two boxes. Very few of us are actually completely one or the other. For example, some people like extreme sports and the thrill of the ride but don't really have an extreme or risk-taking nature. Plenty of extreme athletes and habitual entrepreneurs are deeply faithful to their families, their finances, and their faith. For that matter, plenty of housewives have never even tried an action sport but long for a dangerous romance or other high-risk venture.

But we can acknowledge the limits of categories while still finding them useful. Jesus used pictures and parables— like seeds, candles, coins, and lost sheep—to help us understand our lives better. Not everything about a seed is like the kingdom of God (the kingdom doesn't taste great in granola). Not everything about a lost sheep is like you or me when we're spiritually lost (we don't get sheared to make blankets). But the pictures (visual generalizations) that Jesus used are helpful and memorable, wouldn't you agree? They can help us get our spiritual sight back, and turn our hearts toward hope.

In this chapter, I want to use the two pictures or categories I've described to help us understand the differences between what I call radical (or extreme) and foundational people. And since I'm writing to fellow radicals, if you're a radical person, I want to help you see fresh ways you can succeed in the unique life God made you for—both as an individual and in the relationships that matter to you most.

The Radicals Among Us

The life statement of a truly extreme person might read, "Bring me a good feeling that I can depend on. Bring me someone or something that consistently makes me feel good. *That* is when I feel happy." We like to get an emotional, or better yet, physical, charge out of every area of life. Otherwise, why do it? This applies to our work, our loving relationships, our walk of faith, and our play. It applies to what we drive or ride, to what we read or watch—heck, to what kind of dog we keep around. If the excitement starts to fade in any of these areas, we feel compelled to make a change.

IF THE EXCITEMENT STARTS TO FADE, WE FEEL COMPELLED TO MAKE A CHANGE.

For us radicals who are followers of Jesus, much of our relationship with God tends to be based on how we feel during worship or prayer rather than on a fundamental trust in what the Bible says. At least, that's the risk. We even tend to evaluate others' faith based on their experiences rather than, for example, how well they've thought through their beliefs.

We usually disdain anything that is boring, institutional, "vanilla," heavily monitored, process oriented, or routine. At our best we are entrepreneurs, top salespeople, and innovators of anything old and dry. At our worst we are selfishly independent, addicted to drugs or alcohol, and have a larger amount of broken bones and wounded relationships than average people.

While we battle in many areas, a couple things we do not struggle with are complacency and fear. It's not that we cannot relax or that we do not feel fear. We just tend to process these two common killers in different ways than the average person. Complacency does not really enter the picture because we're always on the move. And fear is used more as a tool than anything else—instead of allowing it to throw us into inaction or "paralysis of analysis," we're more likely to use its energy to change our situations.

Speaking of being on the move, it's hard for us to sit down and read books. Many of us can read three or four books at a time, but most of those books are not usually read from front to back (or finished, for that matter). I have been reading Thomas Freidman's *The World Is Flat*[3] for six months by skipping around the book, picking a chapter here and there, and reading till I get tired and fall asleep. The bathtub at the Barrett house has a tile shelf lined with fifteen books I am at some stage of reading. Most are water damaged by now, having suffered through my "pick up and put down" reading ways for too long. (Some books escape this fate. When I first picked up the John Eldredge book *Wild at Heart*,[4] I knew that it would be a rare book that I would read all the way through.

God used it to begin a long-lasting process of healing in my
life. I have reread parts of the book a few times since, and I
continue to find gold.)

Many people from our unsettled tribe move from job to
job or relationship to relationship. Those closest to us must
be constantly on guard against the next radical decision that
might affect them.

Here's an overview of a radical person's makeup:

RELATIVE STRENGTHS	RELATIVE WEAKNESSES
Not Managed by Fear	Quick-tempered
Welcomes Change	Selfishly Independent
Natural Risk-taker	Tends to Be Irresponsible
Highly Relational	Tends to Be Inconsiderate

Radical Profile

You can see from this chart that life with a radical person is
rarely going to be boring. Unfortunately, it can also be very
painful. Here's a personal example:

At one point in my marriage, I found myself bored and
looking for some adventure to break up the monotony of
work, kids, and bills. So I started to entertain the idea of
reconnecting with an old girlfriend via e-mail. Life needed
more risk and electricity, or so I thought. At the time, I got

excited about the idea of meeting up with her secretly some-day in a faraway place. I began to imagine escaping with her, from time to time, from the trappings of suburban married life.

Looking back on this today, I understand how married people can end up in destructive Internet-based relation-ships. In my case, only a few e-mails had been exchanged before my wife found them on the computer. That began a long and very painful experience for both of us. I cautiously share this story only to make the point that when things get routine or stabilized, highly charged people are more apt to shake things up and hurt those around them in the process. (This is not an excuse for a weak character, but rather an explanation of how we regularly cause heartache. There is no excuse for the foolish things I have done. They are wrong.)

Many extreme people are outstanding peacetime leaders but horrible wartime leaders. Have you noticed how every-one wants to follow a radical person when things are good and happy, probably because they have vision and passion and energy? But when times are bad many of them/us can make impulsive and poor choices that end up hurting people, families, projects, and even companies.

In my opinion, only a small and highly valuable minor-ity of adventure seekers actually get more intelligent under pressure. These people account for some of the best leaders in history. These rare people, whom the Bible refers to as "complete" or "refined," are most valuable during a time of crisis because they have learned to control their behavior and emotions while taking some extraordinary risk to accomplish an important mission. Early in life Theodore Roosevelt had a full-on danger habit; he was a true globe-trotting adventurer who later became an author and accomplished president of the United States. Navy Seals or Green Berets might be examples of extreme people who have disciplined themselves to the point of being stunningly valuable during an intense situation or sustained conflict. They have learned how to wait for the cookie.

But most of us danger seekers just take "stupid pills" and act without thinking. We put out fires with gasoline or escalate a friendly debate into a raging fight. We can thrash people verbally before they have a chance to respond.

Fortunately, there's plenty of good news for the radicals among us too. For example, while we may learn slowly, we tend to learn well. I compare us to how the metal manganese is used in technology. Manganese is an easy-to-find gray-white metal that resembles iron. Little bits of it are hidden in the ground all over the world. When mined in large quantities and processed correctly, it becomes an extremely hard metal that is brittle, easily damaged, and potentially toxic. Without considerable expertise, manganese is difficult to fuse or combine with other metals. (Does this analogy begin to sound familiar?) The real potential for manganese, however, is its ability to greatly strengthen other metals like steel and aluminum. In the rock-crushing industry, a plate of manganese bolted to a rotating lump of steel can crush boulders the size of your house. That is strong stuff!

But here's the best part: The more a manganese plate is hit, the stronger it becomes. Friction and distress actually make it tougher and more useful. I keep that picture in mind

I'M NOT A MISTAKE, AND NEITHER ARE YOU.

when my faults and mistakes begin to get me down. I'm not a mistake, and neither are you. If we allow God to shape our lives, amazing things will happen.

Foundational People

While extreme people base much of their life on feelings and change, foundational people build their lives on dependability. They would most easily identify with this statement: "Bring me something or someone I can believe in; show me what is trustworthy and logical. That is how I experience happiness."

The foundational people I know are usually happier when things are, or feel, stable and secure. They long for things like a good book and long conversation with a close friend. Words like "harmony" and "stability" comfortably roll off their tongue, and they generally seem more adept at listening to what other people are saying. I think they also balance their checkbooks. They can certainly become bored, and they can also take risks and kick a fence or two. But under pressure, they will tend to err on the side of caution.

While younger companies usually look for radical leaders, as organizations mature they tend to choose foundational leadership. This shift toward a steady hand at the helm reminds me of the description of the ideal centurion by the Roman historian, Polybius: "Centurions are desired not to be bold and adventurous so much as good leaders, of steady and prudent mind, not prone to take the offensive or start fighting wantonly, but able when overwhelmed and hard pressed to stand fast and die at their post."

Psalm 12:1 reminds us how valuable foundational people are to the fabric of our families, companies, and society, especially during challenging times: "Help Lord! For principled and godly people are here no more; faithfulness and the faithful vanish from among the sons of men" (AMP).

Here's an overview of a foundational person's makeup:

RELATIVE STRENGTHS	RELATIVE WEAKNESSES
Stable	Resists Taking Risks
Driven by Principles	Reluctant to Be Spontaneous
Patient	Tends to Accept the Status Quo
Consistent and Hard Working	Undervalues Play or Time for Self

Foundational Profile

Recognize anyone in your life in this profile? Most radical people learn early on that a foundational person makes an invaluable partner: in business, in play, in marriage. Otherwise you bounce all your checks, no one wants to organize base camp, and all you have to eat in the house is peanut butter and jelly.

And when was the last time you wanted an adrenaline-fueled risk taker for your tax accountant, lawyer, IT consultant, spiritual director, or neurosurgeon?

The group of people who live within the foundational paradigm help to stabilize and ground the rest of us. My wife, Donna, is cut from this piece of cloth. Over the years I've come to depend on her stability by running ideas past her or asking for her to evaluate perplexing life decisions. Why? Well, on a really tough decision I might take ten minutes to reach closure. She'll take ten days or longer. There have been countless times where I was sure we had moved through the discussion phase and reached a final decision only to find out she was just talking out loud. She was still "chewing" on the idea. I'll admit that this kind of process thinking drives me nuts. I prefer to just make the decision and live with the consequences; it makes life more exciting. But Donna's integrity and thoughtfulness have saved our family a lot of embarrassment (to say nothing of pain, money, and time).

Of course, there's a downside to being foundational or living with someone who is. Sometimes they can slow things down too much. After all, they don't like risk. And they tend to fear the unknown. What can result is "analysis paralysis" because they get stuck in the evaluation process and cannot easily take the risk to break out of it. Sometimes they need a radical nudge to help them get a clear vision of what they want and need, and to take action.

SOMETIMES THEY NEED A RADICAL NUDGE TO HELP THEM GET A CLEAR VISION.

In case I've given the wrong impression, I have met many surfers who like things stable, predictable, and routine. They have no desire to take that much risk, even though they are not afraid to drop into an overhead wave. I have also met mothers, accountants, and librarians who get bored sick with their lives and decide one day to take up skydiving or to solo backpack through Patagonia.

Remolded for Higher Purpose

Whether we're foundational or radical, a fantastic purpose in life awaits us if we're willing to live under the rule of God. If you've been identifying yourself as a radical, with all the privileges and pains pertaining thereto, I want to tell you that you are not some genetic mistake or the permanent victim of a set of bad parents. You have your passions and drives for a good purpose. You have a deep desire to overcome danger, to overcome the fears in your life, for a reason. You even have your weaknesses for a reason, though you probably have a hard time believing that on most days.

Believing in your purpose, and committing yourself to finding it and living it out, is one of the most important journeys in life. That's why, in the pages ahead, I want to help you strike out in new directions that can have a huge and positive impact on your life and on the lives of others around you.

The fact is that in addition to creating us with innate strengths and weaknesses, God also created us to be in motion, to change and grow over time. Call it the road of multiplying effectiveness or diminishing damage or simply the path of wisdom and maturity. Whatever the label, it's a very promising journey for each of us, and yet it's one that few radicals I've met seem to take or even know about. But it's a journey that changes everything, starting with you.

The promise of a life in motion is what I want to delve into in the next chapter.

The Miracle of Movement

Therefore, if anyone is in Christ, he is a new creation;
the old has gone, the new has come!
2 CORINTHIANS 5:17

Do you think people can change? I mean, really? And here's an even tougher question: Do you really believe *you* can change?

Personal change—and the possibility that you and I can choose a higher level of radical living—is what I want to talk about in this chapter. (Right off, let me assure you that I'm not talking about turning you from Radical Reggie into Foundational Frank. Okay, you're wife or girlfriend might want that to happen every now and then, but it isn't going to, and it's not what God wants for you anyway.)

We hear all the time that people never really change. Maybe you've heard the statement: "Show me the child and I will show you the man." And it's true that in our darker moments we're pretty sure we'll always be what we've always been—emotionally driven, stupidness and all. It's also true that a lot about us—our personality type, our genetic makeup, our crooked nose—won't change (without surgery), and probably isn't meant to. But, in another sense, a human being who can't solve problems and adapt and learn isn't much better than a rock.

Every highly trained athlete fine-tunes even the smallest details about his or her workout regimen, diet, sleep, hydration routine, equipment, and on and on. It's all about learning what works, and what doesn't—and making adjustments. Do

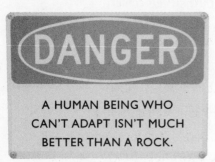

A HUMAN BEING WHO CAN'T ADAPT ISN'T MUCH BETTER THAN A ROCK.

you want to vault higher, jump farther, slalom faster, skate higher? Then you gotta change.

So why is it that so many of us radicals choose the no-change option in our personal lives? We basically say, "Well, I am what I am. Deal with it, baby!" And we keep on saying it while the losses for ourselves and others pile up around us.

Take a moment to ask yourself what kind of internal conversation you've been having on this issue in recent weeks. Where do you tend to land when it comes to personal change? What's your record of trying (and maybe failing) to change? What's your level of desire?

One of the most amazing and compelling dimensions of the teachings of Jesus is His promise that we were actually created for change—good change—and that God Himself is powerfully committed to and involved in the process. Phenomenal. That's why I'm calling this chapter "The Miracle of Movement."

Because when you've proven for years that "Start Over" is your middle name, movement to a healthy and higher functioning you feels like a miracle. I know. Maybe you do too.

Higher, Faster, Better: Profiles of a Life in Motion

If we find ourselves living in a frame that we were not designed for...we need to move! But personal change requires a lot of power. Kurt Lewin, often called the father of social psychology, built a model for change back in the 1930s called the Force Field Analysis. It describes, among other things, how opposing forces in one's life may cause change. In the same way a Mike Tyson punch can change our plans or the way manganese is pounded into something stronger and more useful, opposing forces in our life can cause us to change and move into God's higher purpose for us.

Because something inside our personalities is cemented into our life from birth, it takes a miracle to move someone toward new birth and new life. Only with that miracle of movement, assisted by the Holy Spirit, does life become the journey we have all longed for. Life at its best is a trek from a place of brokenness and wreckage to a place of healing and restoration. Where most of us are today is not our final destination but only a stopping point on the way to our calling. It is the presence and power of Christ in us, and our own choice to follow Him, that propels us through our life's clutter and into our highest and best calling.

I know that change happens. I've seen it. As a pastor I have seen people radically changed, from the inside out, to become someone they never imagined they could be. The most hardened surfers move from drinking and smoking with their buddies every night and battling through anger and rage to becoming softened lovers of God and other people. I have seen fighters become people of peace. Bored, depressed, and confused young women have become champions of faith in their hometown and on the mission field.

I KNOW THAT CHANGE
HAPPENS. I'VE SEEN IT.

Of course, personal movement doesn't come without pain. My friend Ted Gillette is a businessman, a pastor, and surfer. He recently told me about the moment when he began to change, where he moved from a place of brokenness to an accelerated life with Christ. It wasn't easy for him, and it probably would not be easy for you. He was with a friend at a Young Life Christian retreat when he felt a burning inside and the call to leave everything else behind and follow Christ.

"My heart was deeply warmed at that moment, and it was more painful not to follow," he told me. "Since that decisive moment I've sought God's voice and the freedom of His call while casting off tradition. Has it been painful? It always will be, but that's the way of the cross. But I'll tell you, it will never be as painful as denying the cross."

To help you think big about personal change, I need you to think tiny for a minute. I'm talking subatomic tiny…

The Free Radical: A Picture in Molecules

In the year 1900, a Russian named Moses Gomberg discovered the first free radical. He became the founder of what is known today as radical chemistry. As applied to human biology, a free radical is an atomic particle that (unlike stable radicals) has unpaired electrons, which make it highly reactive and unstable. Since Gomberg's time, free radicals have been shown to damage cells or even human DNA, yet we now know they can attack bacteria and even bring healing (for example in countering the neuron damage associated with Alzheimer's disease).

Talk about a paradox. The same tiny particle can take a life…or save a life.

Get the picture?

Aren't we extreme people much the same as we interact

with business colleagues, family, and community? Haven't we protected the weak one day only to bully them the next? The challenge is to channel our power and potential in positive directions. In a very real sense, we need to be "freed for good." We must no longer be subject to our destructive tendencies but released as redeeming agents under the Lordship of Jesus Christ.

If we fail in pursuing this new, life-enhancing direction (which we will at times), God offers an unending supply of grace and miraculous power to bring us back to our feet and put us on the journey again. It's the core message of the gospel of Jesus Christ: The Savior of the world reaches into the lives of each of us, no matter where we are in life, and brings us love and grace and healing. He is always ready to restore us to a loving relationship with Himself.

In his book *The Ragamuffin Gospel*, Brennan Manning so wonderfully articulates God's heart for all of us who fail, and continue to fail, in our quest. He says, "But when we accept ownership of our powerlessness and helplessness, when we acknowledge that we are paupers at the door of God's mercy, then God can make something beautiful out of us."[2]

The alternative to directing our energies toward bringing life and healing isn't pretty. That's because the misdirected extreme life is a dangerous place to live for an extended period of time.

In fact, the more selfish and morally bankrupt the person is, the more dangerous they become. We all know people with level-ten intensity who show a one or two on the morality and selflessness scales. Like a rogue free radical, that person is surrounded by "tissue damage" in their relationships and their jobs, and to some innocent people around them who were unlucky enough to cross their path on the wrong day.

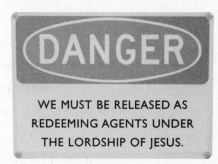

WE MUST BE RELEASED AS REDEEMING AGENTS UNDER THE LORDSHIP OF JESUS.

The worst-case scenario is when this person does not realize how selfish or impulsive they are, and they wake up one day feeling they have no more value in this life. Those closest to them have left. Everything looks like it is ruined and the opportunity for a fulfilling life is disappearing fast.

The Bible puts a name to the picture of choosing the radical life without harnessing it to God's plans. Maybe you've heard it.

The Trapped Radical: A Picture in Muscles

Samson might still be the poster boy for danger addicts, even though he lived three thousand years ago. Every kid dreaming of making it in the WWE wants to be the next Samson. The name, like Hercules in Greek mythology, stands for *raw power, huge muscles,* and *incredible feats of daring.*

What most kids don't know is that the name could also stand for incredible opportunities incredibly wasted.

According to the Bible, God chose Samson before he was born and gave him an unusual sensitivity to the Holy Spirit (see Judges 13:24–25), then blessed him with amazing gifts and abilities. So amazing that he would have made a sweep of pretty much any extreme sport he entered. It's clear from the Bible account that God had a heroic plan for Samson's life. The nation of Israel was in a dark time; they kept getting beat up by their enemies.

Enter God's ripped and fearless strong man. Over the course of his life, Samson:

- killed a lion with his bare hands (Judges 14:6);
- killed a thousand enemy soldiers using only a donkey's jawbone for a weapon (Judges 15:14–16);
- tore a locked, barred city gate off its hinges with his bare hands—then carried it to the top of a nearby hill just for spite (Judges 16:3); and
- made a heathen temple collapse, killing thousands by single-handedly pushing down it's supporting pillars. (vv. 23–30)

Just looking over his bio you get a strong sense that Samson loved a good fight, enjoyed bad odds, and didn't mind making a show of his strength either! He was a man driven by his passions. But his passions came with a dark side. The *Zondervan Bible Dictionary* nails his extreme nature when it says this about Samson: "But almost from the beginning of his career he showed one conspicuous weakness, which was ultimately to wreck him: He was a slave to passion."[3]

Samson's craving for risk and addiction to anger and lust drove him to pick fights when he didn't need to, to look inside the enemy camp for his girlfriends, and eventually to risk everything he'd accomplished in his life just so he could enjoy the favors of the prostitute Delilah.

It was a risk that cost him his reputation and his life.

The irony of Samson's life is that his unusual strengths could not free him from his own failings. Despite his muscles, the Bible's strong man en-dures through history as a sad example of a trapped radical.

I have to say, though, that I like Samson. I recognize him. He's me (though I don't have quite the muscle mass). And his life reminds me that the first enemy we have to overcome is not the one coming at us with sword or tank, but the one we live with every day—the one inside.

IT WAS A RISK THAT COST HIM HIS REPUTATION AND HIS LIFE.

Who's the Real Enemy of Your Potential?

I was reading recently how Mahatma Ghandi, former political and spiritual leader in India, led that nation through the process of gaining independence from Great Britain. He believed one of the biggest challenges to the independence movement in India was not the British but the mindset of most Indians themselves. He recognized how most Indians had such a low opinion of themselves that many believed they *deserved* to be ruled by the British. Unfortunately for the Indians, the British knew how they felt, and used their attitudes against them.

The British presence amounted to scattered governors and pockets of military troops; India was a sprawling, culturally rich nation of hundreds of millions of people. Describing Britain's power move, Ghandi said that never had a nation ruled over so many with so few. So he set out to show India a different way of thinking, one that spoke into their souls and called them to greatness. The eventual outcome was India's successful move to national independence in 1948.

The same applies to those of us who have settled for a life of addiction, boredom, selfishness, rage, bitterness, depression, or repeated foolishness. Before we can move toward freedom and purpose in our life, like India, we have to first realize that so much of our life has been ruled by so little.

If you have Samson blood pumping in your veins, I can just imagine you are saying things like, "But I just can't control myself!" Or, "Well, I want to change, but I keep getting thrashed by some demon."

On the subject of Satan, let's clear up some misconceptions about spiritual warfare and fighting against the dark forces of evil. I believe that Satan and his demons exist and play a destructive role in this world. But in nearly every case, most of us from Samson's tribe aren't fighting some darker power from the underworld. We're just unwilling to grow up and take responsibility for our own habits and choices.

As a pastor I have had people tell me that Satan is coming against them all the time, making them sick or making their family critical of them, or whatever. I think they just need to eat healthier, exercise, get more rest, and treat people better. Honestly, I don't think it is Satan at all. I think 80 percent of their issues will clear up if they just stop being stupid and start being nicer to people.

Not what you wanted to hear, I know.

If you are not convinced, why not apply some math to the question. We know that the Bible says one-third of the angels fell from heaven, along with Satan, and it is they who get blamed for more than what is deserved. Satan is not omniscient (all-knowing) or omnipresent (everywhere at the same time) or omnipotent (all-powerful all the time) like God is. He is a created being doing the best he can to mess up the program, and I believe God allows him to do that.

Logically and biblically, the Satan described in Scripture takes on people who are, or could be, doing great things for the kingdom of God. Satan somehow got Peter to tell Jesus He should not take the path of a martyr (Matthew 16:21–23). Satan tried to get Jesus to bow down to him or eat bread rather than fast and depend on God's Word alone for His sustenance (Matthew 4:2–4). Satan attacked the apostle Paul with a "thorn in his flesh," which God used to

MOST OF US FROM SAMSON'S TRIBE ARE JUST UNWILLING TO GROW UP.

keep Paul humble and dependent on His grace (2 Corinthians 12:7–9). Satan influenced Ananias and Sapphira, people of influence, wealth, and some faith, to lie to the early church in an effort to infiltrate the church with sin and slow a rapidly growing movement (Acts 5:1–10). There is no biblical or historical reason to think Satan has wasted his time, or intends to waste his time, with people who are no threat or not doing anything for God.

Suffice it to say, if you or I get caught in a hamster wheel of meaningless activity, the fight is probably not against Satan. More likely, it's against our own attitudes, actions, habits, or conflicting desires.

Neither is our fight against God, no matter what we might imagine in the middle of some dark night. The Bible makes it clear that God never leads us astray. The apostle James wrote:

> When tempted, no one should say, "God is tempting me." For God cannot be tempted by evil, nor does he tempt anyone; but each one is tempted when, by his own evil desire, he is dragged away and enticed. Then, after desire has conceived, it gives birth to sin;

and sin, when it is full-grown, gives birth to death.
(James 1:13–15)

Which brings us to the greatest single hope you and I
have for positive motion in our lives.

You Are Hunted

For the last four thousand years, in many ways and in many
languages, Jehovah has told us all that each one of us is
immensely important to Him. We must realize our incredible,
personal value to Him. Since He first imagined our lives
before time began, God has pursued us and fought for our
destiny. We are all hunted men and women!

Look at these amazing Bible texts:

Behold what manner of love the Father has [given]
us, that we should be called children of God.
(1 John 3:1, NKJV)

Jehovah [has] been mindful of us; He will bless us.
(Psalm 115:12, ASV)

And these lines from Psalm 139:

You have hedged me behind and before,
And laid Your hand upon me.

Where can I go from Your Spirit?
Or where can I flee from Your presence? (vv. 5, 7, NKJV)

How supremely wonderful is that? He is mindful of our problems. He is mindful of our dreams. He is mindful of our wounds. He is mindful of our sins. He is mindful of our victories. He is mindful of the times we gave up. He is mindful of the days we stood and fought the good fight. He is mindful of what He created us to be. All in all God is at all times and in every situation mindful of you.

He really did it—sacrificed and suffered on the cross on your behalf, I mean. He really does love you that much. That fact should first cause us to be humble. Then it should cause us to get on our feet and fight for our potential.

With God's relentless pursuit of my heart and mind, a few necessary miracles, and a lot of prayer, I know that I am moving slowly and purposefully toward the freed radical zone. It's what I want for my own life, and what I pray for yours. To settle for anything less would be to be stamped with a very restrictive label, to live out a cartoon (you see 'em all over TV and the movies). Sure, an unmolded radical is nearly always interesting and often dangerous. But ultimately that lifestyle reveals itself to be self-obsessed, hurtful, and small.

And you and I were put on earth for so much more.

It is a miracle when people really change from the inside out. It is that same miracle that you and I still need today. I have zero desire to stay where I am as a husband, a surfer, a father, a businessman, a pastor, or a friend. I want to be moved by God into the zone where great things can happen inside each part I play. And when, like Samson, I get trapped in my own sinful and selfish crap, I hope and pray that God will move me, yet again, to a place where He can redeem the mistakes and bring me new life.

Move us, Lord.

It's Called "Adventure Faith"

Whoever desires to save his life will lose it,
but whoever loses his life for My sake will find it.
JESUS, IN MATTHEW 16:25, NKJV

Everyone wants an adventure. In fact, I can't think of anyone who doesn't like a good, almost impossible challenge now and then, even people who usually keep their lives neat and tidy. The base camp of Mount Everest is filled with doctors, lawyers, accountants, and hairdressers who are willing to pay almost any price for their fifteen minutes on the top.

For some of us, the more dangerous the assignment the more likely we are to join up. In the days of the opening of the West, I would have signed up for the Lewis and Clark expedition. Later, I would have happily pioneered the Oregon Trail. I think the Pony Express would have offered the perfect ride. Those horsemen carried the U.S. Mail across the wild frontier without protection or rest. Most people don't realize the Pony Express lasted less than two years before telegraph wires made it obsolete. But between April of 1860 and November of 1861, America fell in love with the glory and danger they saw in this young, fast group of riders.

To me, it sounds like a dream job. In fact, let me tell you a bit more. Pony Express riders galloped up to seventy-five miles per day, changing mounts as they went, never stopping long enough to sleep, fight, or cook a meal until they were done with their leg of the journey. They rode with only a sack of flour, some bacon, and cornmeal for food. For medical needs they carried nothing more than borax and turpentine. In 1860 a San Francisco newspaper ran an ad for applicants:

"Wanted: Young, skinny, wiry fellows not over 18 years old. Must be excellent riders. Willing to live at risk daily. Orphans preferred."

Despite the risks, low pay, and hard work, the Pony Express was never short of applicants. The reason is simple: People want—and radical people absolutely need—an adventure.

In this chapter I want to address a big idea that may seem alien to you. You may have never heard it or imagined it before. Or if you have, you may have resisted for all you're worth. It's the big idea at the core of this book, and one we'll return to in various ways in the pages ahead. Here it is:

You and I have been created for a leap off the edge, a trek into the wilds, an adventure of a lifetime. And our traveling partner—should we accept the invitation to the adventure—is God Himself.

For a few years now I have called this trek into the wilds with God "adventure faith." I have been blogging on the concept for a couple years, articulating my way through content that I've now woven into this book. I believe this kind of adventure is the thrill you've been looking for, and—good news for adrenaline junkies everywhere—it comes complete with maximum cost and risk. For example, you will get rejected. You will suffer physically and emotionally. You may fail disastrously. You will face the greatest opponent known to man...

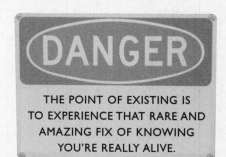

THE POINT OF EXISTING IS TO EXPERIENCE THAT RARE AND AMAZING FIX OF KNOWING YOU'RE REALLY ALIVE.

And there's more good news: You will say, maybe for the first time, "This is the life I was meant to live!"—which is the point of existing, isn't it? Experiencing firsthand that rare and amazing fix of knowing you're really, fully, this very minute...alive.

Three Yards and a Cloud of Dust

You might remember hearing about the day the apostle Paul's adventure began. He was on his way to find more Christians to persecute when he got knocked to the ground by the presence and power of Jesus. That encounter brought about a dramatic course correction. "Now get up and go into the city, and you will be told what you must do," Jesus told him (Acts 9:6). He obeyed, and the early church—and the world—was never the same.

In the Old Testament, David's adventure began when he was a young man alone tending his father's sheep. Without warning, the prophet Samuel called him out of the fields and anointed him to be Israel's future king (1 Samuel 16:11–13). That one day changed almost everything about his future. Just ask Goliath.

But what about you and me? Where does our adventure begin? Even though you and I were created to want and need adventure, that doesn't mean we should just go out and make one happen. (That is what we have done, mostly unsuccessfully, for years.) It looks great in the scrapbooks, it sells magazines and enhances television ads, but it leaves our soul dry and empty. If we are trying to follow the person and teachings of Jesus, then it's wiser to wait and pray for His guidance. He knows our needs (He made us). A better idea, even though it's not easy, is to stop running for a change and wait.

From my personal experience, I can tell you that He will lead us onto good paths. Sometimes, though, the path is long, and the wait for His change is painful. And for some of us, it takes a lot of hard knocks before we realize that the right change for us lies in God's hands, not ours.

Some years ago I could have never dreamed up the mission God had in store for me and my family. As a father of four with a big mortgage payment and a twenty-two-minute commute to the office, things looked pretty normal. But underneath that veneer we were slowly morphing into a lifestyle that even our children hated. No offense, but I can't think of anything more boring than a thirty-eight-year-old Christian husband of a really nice wife and four average kids who piles his family into the minivan every Sunday morning at 9:45 and heads to church. (After the weekly Sunday morning argument, of course. At least that part was not boring.)

The half-lived life of an American Christian male walked past me on Main Street every day. In fact, it was me, and I hated it. I remember thinking I only needed one thing from God: to better understand my wife. Our relationship suffered from daily fights and a growing distance. Neither of us was happy and both of us later admitted to thoughts of leaving.

I did my best to bring healthy changes, with mixed results. For example, with good-hearted Christian ambition, I started an Alpha Group in our home. We invited non-Christian friends and businesspeople for dinner and discussions about Christianity. It was an eight-week program that was supposed to result in some people deciding to try God and church on for size. It was billed as a professional and intelligent person's bridge to the church. It was a great program, and we built some deeper friendships with our non-Christian friends. But nobody from that group ever tried church, and nobody changed their belief system.

Next, I tried to help some unemployed people in our church find work. I put together a networking and resume-building class. I think we called it "How to Get a Job," and we set it up as a small group through my church. After eight weeks of effort, networking, and coaching (from me, of course) nobody got a new job. Not one person gained anything from the effort.

Near the bottom of my own spiritual journey, I thought about going to extreme measures to save my life from going down some meaningless, pathetic path. One friend told me that I was like "three yards and a cloud of dust," meaning that I had a lot of flash at first only to fizzle out after a few yards. At around that same time, one of my pastors at the Portland Vineyard Church, Wally Moore, told me he used to help build dragsters when he was a teenager. He said there is a lot of science and engineering that goes into setting the ratios between engine weight and tire traction. It is possible, he said, to build a race car that is so powerful in the engine that the wheels only spin out and leave a lot of smoke and rubber behind. There is no real forward momentum that takes full advantage of the engine's power. Sitting on the banks of the slow-moving Tualatin River and drinking lattes together one day, he told me that reminded him of me. In a very loving and brutal way, he said I was like that poorly built race car—a lot of engine power but not really going anywhere.

I HAD A LOT OF FLASH AT FIRST ONLY TO FIZZLE OUT AFTER A FEW YARDS...

I left that conversation knowing I really was "three yards and a cloud of dust." For all my efforts, I was mostly just stirring up a lot of commotion and a bad smell.

Pressing into the Truth

About that time, a friend of mine told me about his experiences with fasting and how it opened his eyes to deeper things about God and life. That sounded like a good idea to me. After all, it was an ancient and proven discipline for the most spiritually committed people on earth, and if I was ever going to count myself among them, I better try it. Besides, my marriage was hurting. I thought maybe if I fasted and prayed for a few days I could gain some supernatural insight into how *she* thinks and what *she* expects from me. That way I could help *her* change.

After just a day and a half of fasting, my expectations began to shift. Instead of getting clarity on my wife's problems, I began noticing serious contradictions in my own life.

Maybe there are things about me that need to be changed, I thought. By the end of the three days, I was rocked by the insights the Holy Spirit was granting me. For example, that I was a fake. Almost everything about my work and family life had developed a false veneer. In several important areas, I was even a fake Christian and a fake husband.

During those days and weeks of praying and fasting, I discovered that God doesn't deny the power of His Spirit when we are committed enough to press into the truth. I came away with an overwhelming desire to be authentic—in everything I do, in everything I am. I began to notice things in me and around me that were false. I could spot another pretender a mile away as he or she began to posture in ways I always did.

ALMOST EVERYTHING ABOUT
MY WORK AND FAMILY LIFE HAD
DEVELOPED A FALSE VENEER.

At the time a friend was moving out of an addiction to drugs and pornography. I remember thinking that he was so much more screwed up than me. *I am so glad that I don't have his problems*, I thought. But on a drive from Boise to Portland, we talked for hours. That's when I started to realize that, like him, I was also in recovery. God was helping me to move out of a life of addiction to risk and pretending to be someone I was not. We both laughed and cried as we realized how raw we were before God and how much He desired our complete surrender to His rule in our lives.

Then, to make matters worse, my small business began to unravel. Initially, my company had grown fast by building sales teams around the country for venture-funded technology start-ups. But after the dot-com crash and some bad decisions on my part, we began to lose customers and cash. In the end, I closed down the business and filed for bankruptcy. I had to terminate the employment of close friends and let investors know I had lost their money and there was nothing more I could do.

In all this hardship, I was more raw, and more honest about who I really was than any other time in my life. But the pain of failure and a slowly growing desire for maturity in Christ helped me during that time to take more steps to put my life in God's hands. And as I did, my own miracle of movement began to happen.

After the business failed, I decided not to make a move unless I sensed God's voice and direction. I moved more slowly and prayed about everything before I did it. If my pastor asked me to lead a Bible study, I'd pray about it first.

I started to pray more about my future too. I asked God to show me how to live my life in His plan instead of my own. I wanted His adventure, not mine. I wanted to learn to serve others without asking for something in return, even appreciation. I wanted to do it because that was the right and honest thing to do. Slowly, God began to uproot some of the selfishness in my personality. As strange as it sounds, I even became more concerned about the planet, the environment, and how I treated my own pets.

Praying for His Adventure

But, true to form, after getting a steady job as a technology sales and marketing guy, I started getting antsy again. I needed to get back in the race and run with my regenerated faith, but this time I wanted the correct ratio between the engine and the tires. So I prayed. Donna and I wanted to try another Alpha Group in our home, but we didn't sense the *yes* from God that we were looking for.

Another close friend, Victor Anfuso, used to tell me that the Bible verse "Let the peace of God rule in your hearts" (Colossians 3:15, NKJV) meant more than most people think. He said the word "rule" in the English Bible comes from a Greek word that means "umpire." He explained how God's peace acts like an umpire for those who are making decisions in their Christian life: "If you have His peace in your heart, then God is behind your decision; if you don't, then God is not in it."

So that is what Donna and I set out to find—God's peace in our hearts for some type of service in the kingdom of God.

As an occasional reader of *Surfer* magazine, I had noticed an ad about Christian Surfers United States. More out of curiosity than anything else, I went to their website and downloaded their "New Chapter Start-up Kit." Starting a chapter for CSUS was something I was praying about, but I didn't really take it too seriously. The reason was, I loved surfing too much. No kidding. I thought starting a Christian surf club or CSUS chapter was selfish, so I avoided the idea for almost a year, all the while thinking God must want me to do something more, well…normal. How could anything related to surfing be that spiritual—especially for a businessman with a wife and kids?

The desire to serve God was so strong in me that I would have done anything He asked, even if it was something completely boring and routine, which is what I expected. That is why, when I kept running into surfers in strange places and in divine ways, I was shocked. While praying about how to serve God the way He wanted, I would coincidently meet surfers on airplanes to Chicago or at a Starbucks in Portland and the conversation would strangely turn itself toward the CSUS idea.

Besides learning to trust God enough to seek His best during this time, I was also learning new ways to communicate with Him. Praying had always been such a formulaic endeavor for me, picked up from years of Sunday school and canned prayers at church. But I was beginning to see prayer differently. One day while thinking about my prayer habits, I realized there was a pattern developing:

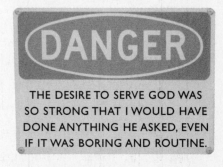

THE DESIRE TO SERVE GOD WAS SO STRONG THAT I WOULD HAVE DONE ANYTHING HE ASKED, EVEN IF IT WAS BORING AND ROUTINE.

Step One: Pray for my requests. Family, money, church, community, praises, etc.

Step Two: Stop praying when I have nothing more to say.

Step Three: Start reading the Bible for my answers.

I got to wondering how the process might work if I communicated with my wife in the same way.

Step One: Call Donna's answering machine and leave a long message telling her stuff and asking for things.

Step Two: Stop talking when I'm done and hang up.

Step Three: Go read some old letters between us to find the answers to my questions.

Okay, it's not an exact analogy because the living Word of God is inspired, and our old letters are just inspiring, but, well, you get the point. I did not dialogue with my Lord or dream with my Lord or wait in silence to hear my Lord speak back to me. To tell you the truth, waiting on God isn't any easier for me than waiting on anything else in life. I just want to get going. Five minutes of silence feels like a lifetime. After I got a high-speed Internet connection at my home I couldn't bring myself to use dial-up again. So how am I supposed to wait for the unseen God to respond to me during prayer?

If you knew me well you would realize that I'm still working on waiting. But it helps to remember who is King in this conversation, and who is the broken, needy, often-forgiven servant.

Giving Up Everything

Knowing how much I love to surf, Donna asked me one night why I was not pursuing the CSUS ministry. "Why would God give you so much passion for something and ask you not to use it?" she asked. "What if that is the exact path He wants you to take?"

Her comment stunned me. I was willing to walk away from my own life and desires to pursue anything that God wanted from me. But could it be possible that God was handing it back to me? I contemplated this verse in Matthew: "He who has the desire to keep his life will have it taken from him, and he who gives up his life because of me will have it given back to him" (v. 10:39, BBE).

A few months later I set out to start an Oregon chapter of Christian Surfers United States. We held our first meeting at the Lincoln City Surf Shop on the Oregon Coast in March of 2003. There were only five of us, but by the end of that first summer our numbers had grown to more than twenty-five at Bible studies, and more than a hundred surfers coming to the monthly surf events. Best of all, God was bringing hardened antichurch surfers to Himself. Within two years, we had a full-time chapter director, Jason Menke, who raised his own financial support and helped start Bible studies in three different Oregon cities. Hundreds of surfers were being reached through surf contests, e-mail newsletters, and mission trips— remarkable in a state with perhaps only five thousand surfers altogether. So God's hand was all over this.

Things kept changing fast. One of the Christian Surfers who came to some of our events was a pastor of a small beach church who needed a sabbatical. I agreed to share a Bible message for a few Sundays to help out, and things grew, friendships grew, and our love for the people of this small church grew. So after a year, we sold our home in the suburbs and moved to the Oregon Coast where I became the full-time teaching pastor. Today, my career in global technology consulting continues to grow. At the same time I remain the volunteer teaching pastor of this small beach church, and I now serve on the national board of directors for Christian Surfers United States. Can you see how the tires began to grab hold?

DANGER

ALL ADVENTURES WORTH
THEIR SALT CONTAIN BOTH
THE MOUNTAINS AND VALLEYS.

This ongoing adventure has lifted and inspired my family beyond anything I could have imagined. My kids and I surf together around the world. The expedition that God has designed for us has wandered its way through Australia, Brazil, Europe, El Salvador, Mexico, Canada, India, and across both coasts of the U.S. Each trip has brought divine appointments and thrilling times in the Spirit. Some have also been host to failure and sin. But all adventures worth their salt contain both the mountains and valleys. By definition, it comes with the territory.

Your Own Adventure Faith

As you think back over your story—the spiritual and emotional journey that has brought you to this page—would you say you have opened yourself to the possibility of a life adventure with God? Or would you say you've taken about every risk (including a ton of boneheaded ones) *except* the "adventure faith" I've been talking about?

I invite you to process this question in your own way, in your own time. No decision makes any sense if it doesn't come out of your authentic life and values. There's no rush. But I believe the Holy Spirit brought you to these pages to encounter a very tantalizing possibility. If you're open to getting more pura vida out of your risk-taking, the Spirit will continue to guide your passions and your thoughts.

I can tell you that our family has certainly found our own adventure in faith on the Oregon Coast. We are conscious of the mission here, and with our best efforts we are committed to it for as long as He desires. With as much grace and forgiveness as He provides, we try to follow the person and teachings of Jesus no matter what we are functionally doing for Him. Surfing ministry, business deals, home Bible study groups, overseas missions—whatever it is, He is able to carry us through anything and direct us into anything. It is thrilling. It is somewhat scary. It is altogether an adventure with our Creator.

As I alluded to above, there is a downside to every adventure for sure. For example, our adventure is certainly not some TV preachers' idea of the wealthy and healthy. We could also end up with our metaphorical boat run aground for awhile by an illness, financial pain, or something worse.

I want my family to live comfortably, and I want my kids to go to college. I also want us to live every day with the anticipation that God could take us anywhere and have us do anything that He desires. My family knows that our lives are in the hands of a radical God who could require something wonderful from us tomorrow morning.

You can find your role in this cosmic adventure through deep, authentic prayer and your own willingness to walk away from everything in life that takes a higher position than Christ alone.

Willing to ride fast and hard for the biggest cause imaginable? Ready to live at risk daily? Want to be finally, fully alive?

Then you may be ready to sign up for your own God-given adventure faith.

Chapter
5

We Were Made to Connect

Two are better than one…
For if they fall, one will lift up his companion.
But woe to him who is alone when he falls.
ECCLESIASTES 4:9–10, NKJV

I guess for me, it's all about who I take on the journey with me—
my buddies, my wife, my God. They challenge me so that I
may grow. I grow so that I may lead. I lead so that I may challenge.
I challenge so others may help me find myself.
MARK, A BLOGGER FROM QUARTZ HILL, CALIFORNIA

Look at how many people you talk to on any given day, how many calls you return, or how many names you have on speed dial, and you're likely to think you have a thousand friends. But conversations and acquaintances are not the same thing as quality relationships. And sometimes the danger tribe doesn't notice until it's too late.

What does it mean to be connected to other people? How important is it, especially for the radically independent types? And how do we make it happen? That's what I want us to explore in this chapter.

Of course, there is something beautiful about the loner life. "Wild and independent" is something we picked up from our sports and media heroes. And for many of us, quick connections happen easily. On short notice, we can be at "life of the party" level or build rapport with strangers (especially if we want something from them). But slowing down and committing ourselves to really knowing someone is tougher. And often, we don't even want to. The life of the loner seems to be working for us just fine.

In the States, we get to pursue the ruggedly individual life as much as we want. We proudly say, "I live in a free country, so I am free to do and be what I want."

How cool is that?

And, ultimately, how deadly?

The problem isn't being rugged, of course, or even being a rugged individualist. That really is kinda cool. But sometimes that attitude turns into our religion. At its extreme, we prize personal freedom above almost everything else.

Above loyalty.

Above commitments.

Above responsibilities.

Above family.

Above...

The whole time we're going after our perfect right to one more thrill, the wife and kids are at home waiting, the credit cards are maxed, and our longtime neighbors hardly recognize us anymore.

The first five years of my marriage to Donna were filled with times where I would just leave the house and go surfing without saying anything to anyone. Or I'd have coffee with a friend for hours, never letting her know where I was or with whom. I wasn't pimping myself around town or hiding in the back of some bar; I was just living my normal life, the kind of life Tigger might live in the Hundred Acre Wood. And the problem was, I thought that was normal.

But that kind of thinking doesn't work in the long haul.

Extreme people I've known tell me they recognize the pattern—and the problem. We wander in our loner universe effortlessly (hey, we're good at it). Before long, though, we experience isolation and separation from family, friends, neighbors, our community, and even from our God. In some cases we can develop a secret life that's killing us, and no one even knows. Sure, we might be rubbing shoulders with people every day—working, playing, doing business, and going to church with them. But we're still alone. Still calling all the empty shots. Our universe still revolves around only one person.

No matter how good it feels on the front end, ultimately, there's a huge personal cost. It doesn't matter if we are talking about golfers, kayakers, fishermen, or surfers. Something more eternal and something more wonderful is missing when we make a lifestyle out of rushing out the front door and strapping the gear on the Yakima racks with no plans to return until late Sunday night ("Don't wait up, honey"). We can't build genuine friendships that way. We can't build lasting family or community ties. But we don't have to get stuck in that lifestyle if we're willing to lay aside some bad habits and old assumptions, take the time to care and listen, and begin to dump a lot of pride and selfishness.

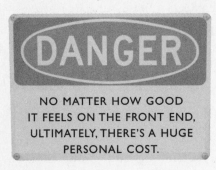

NO MATTER HOW GOOD IT FEELS ON THE FRONT END, ULTIMATELY, THERE'S A HUGE PERSONAL COST.

In this chapter I want to look at the risks of the loner life (it's hugely oversold). And I want to propose that you and I are made for something better and more rewarding. Because like every other human on the planet, we have been created by God for more than one person. We were made for community.

We were made to connect.

The Family Connection

My friend Corey Wells, a surfer, graphic designer, father, and husband, told me one day: "I think to live your life anywhere *but* on the edge is a waste, but I'm the first to tell you, I have tamed myself in the past years mainly because I am more aware of my family."

Family changes things for extreme people—and that's a good thing. When the surf is good, guys like Corey go nuts if they go antique shopping with their wives. Okay, he says it can feel at the time like undergoing a root canal without drugs. But I respect radicals who have learned how to do marriage and family in unique ways. Most of us aren't wired for nest-building and hand-holding our way through life with another person. Something about that closeness, or the responsibilities that come with it, makes us nervous. At least it does me.

Sometimes, when I feel "obligated" to spend a day with the wife and kids, I feel this invisible gate closing and locking in on me. We radicals think, What if the surf never gets this good again? Ahhhh! No more me! (Seriously, we may fear annihilation of ourselves at a very deep level.) So we resist, sneak around, cheat, create conflict (for a margin of safety and privacy), hold back private areas and private passions.

Even as I write I recognize how sick this is. How many of the deep, wonderful things about our family have I missed?

In the book of 1 Timothy, the apostle Paul writes, "If any-one does not provide for [take care of]...his...family, he...is worse than an unbeliever" (v. 5:8). He writes this to a young pastor, no doubt a radical in his time because he was preaching and teaching about Christ in a time and place where they killed you for that. Yet Paul tells him, in effect, that anyone who rejects his responsibilities to care for his family is worse than a person who rejects Christ. That is a shotgun blast of truth in the gut for those of us who never worry where our next meal comes from. And Paul is writing about much more than just financial provision—we are called by God to care for, protect, nurture, and serve our family.

Why? For their good, of course. But for ours too. The idea that we're wandering heroes in our own loner universe is a lie. We're connected. We're part of a larger organism. And we need it. We never achieve our potential, or realize

WE'RE CONNECTED.
AND WE NEED IT.

the full benefit of what God wants to give us, until we slow down, make a commitment to those who depend on us, and say, "I choose this. These people are part of my world and my adventure too. This is what it means to be 100 percent alive."

Rope, Harness, Cams

Remember the friend of mine who told me I was like "three yards and a cloud of dust"? That really hurt me at the time. It hurt so much worse because I knew deep down that it was true. I had to change. And I did. But I know this for a fact: Change never would have happened if Vic had not had the courage to say what he said, and if we didn't have a connection where I listened carefully to what he said.

Friendships on that level must be intentional, I think. They rarely happen by accident. Why? For one thing, wanting or being comfortable with the idea of open, honest, accountable friendships goes against the basics of the radical personality.

Listen to conversations at the mall, surfshop, or the local bar and you notice, just under the surface of small talk and jokes and stories, something pretty sobering: a tremendous lack of realness among the friends. Think of the last ten conversations you had with your closest friends. Did you talk about what you fear most? Did you lay out the areas in your life where you feel waves of shame or guilt? Did you talk about your "calling" in life—the direction or purpose you think God put you on earth for?

And how did you invest in their lives? Did you invite them to be totally real with you? Did you look for what you could say or do that might help them turn an important corner? Was anyone challenged to walk away from an addiction, raise a moral standard, or follow through on a deep spiritual commitment? Sure, you heard what they were saying, but did you really listen?

Friendships like I'm talking about are like high-strength rope and hardware systems that climbers use. You can count on them. They hold, no matter how hard you fall, no matter what stupid step you take, no matter how far down it is to bottom.

I was about thirty when I decided to do a solo rock climb

inside the Owens River Gorge on the eastern side of the Sierra Nevadas. I was driving back from a men's Christian retreat at Mammoth Mountain. It was a Sunday afternoon and shade was starting to settle into the Owens River Valley to cool off the rock and make a climbing attempt more possible.

Solo climbing is using all the usual gear (rope, harness, hardware) without the benefit of a climbing partner. At the time I did not think about the fact that nobody else was climbing that day, or that I had no cell phone reception, or that I hadn't climbed solo before.

I had chosen a simple (5.7 or 5.8) route that would accept my three-inch cams placed strategically in the cracks as I ascended. I don't remember now if I had a backup rope in tow, nor do I remember if I used a prusick hitch knot or a Grigri soloist device for protection—I don't remember how prepared I really was.

But I do remember a horrifying fall.

I had climbed about thirty feet up, and I had only placed two cams in the crack for protection. When I fell, the lower cam pulled out of the rock crack and slid down my rope to the valley floor. I felt it pop out, and I turned to see it hit with a cloud of dust at the bottom. This left me hanging thirty feet up by one small cam. My heart was pounding out of my chest as I slowly added another piece of protection and lowered myself to the ground. All the way down I prayed that God would forgive all my sins and cussed myself out for being so stupid.

I left two expensive cams in the crack above me and walked back to the car very disappointed.

But I learned something. It had been extremely stupid to attempt that rock face in those circumstances alone. I needed more protection. I needed a partner with expert, caring eyes, someone to say, "Mike, don't climb that. You're not ready."

In our lives as radicals in pursuit of God's best, we need partners. The reason? Falling is not a maybe but a certainty. It's guaranteed to happen. If your own self-obsessions or the enemy of your soul can isolate you and pull you away from Christian accountability, then you are literally hanging out there alone. No hardware. No backup. No protection.

We need each other. Meaningful friendships—people who understand us, who we invest in, who invest in us—help keep us safe and on the right track. The more you "clip in" along your route, the safer you'll be when you fall. And real friends help us get up again when we blow it.

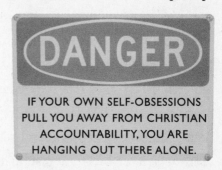

IF YOUR OWN SELF-OBSESSIONS PULL YOU AWAY FROM CHRISTIAN ACCOUNTABILITY, YOU ARE HANGING OUT THERE ALONE.

King Solomon may have had this principle in mind when he wrote about a good person's rebounding ability:

For though a righteous man falls seven times, he rises again, but the wicked are brought down by calamity. (Proverbs 24:16)

In this verse, we should read "wicked" as "loner," as "great guy who makes a foolish, hasty, self-centered choice," as "rugged individualist." Because "wicked" sneaks up on even the best of us if we're not careful.

In a span of only one week, the 2006 round of assaults on Mount Everest brought us remarkable news about great guys who made either just or wicked choices. Here is what happened:

While a fifty-year-old climber, Lincoln Hall, was left for dead by his team, and other passing climbers, a small U.S. team led by Dan Mazur stopped to help him down the mountain. In the process they gave up their own assent.

Weeks later, the guide who led the rescue told *The Today Show*, "We just immediately sprung into action. You have to move quickly up there. If you mess around and start thinking about what to do, he could already be gone."

But this story of heroism and self-sacrifice contrasted with its evil-cousin story that took place only days earlier on the same mountain. Thirty-four-year-old David Sharp died after forty climbers passed him and refused to help. Mark Inglis told a New Zealand TV station that he passed Sharp and radioed for help, but a fellow mountaineer told him: "Look, mate, you can't do anything. You know, he's been there too long without oxygen—you know, he's effectively dead." Had Inglis not been a double amputee, the first to climb Everest, he reported he would have helped Sharp.

One climber is left for dead, but is rescued and lives.

Another is left alone to die...and dies. This is fascinating to me.

The striking phrase in the second story is "effectively dead." Because Sharp was judged "effectively dead," he was treated as though he were actually dead. But you and I know the truth. David Sharp was left to die so that other climbers could complete their ascent.

This story hits home in many ways. First, I am not unlike the dozens of climbers who passed up the dying man. Like each of those climbers, my radical mind has a hard time giving up something I am striving to accomplish or overcome. Doesn't matter, really, if we are climbing Everest or tow-surfing twenty-five-foot waves—we're on a mission to overcome our fear and successfully reach our goal of euphoric accomplishment. Even if someone is dying as we pass.

When I posted the Everest story on my blog, I received this honest and profound response from Mark in Quartz Hill, California:

> Thanks, Mike, for posting this story. The pursuit of the summits in life is where life is lived for me. The journey, between safety and the moment of definition, is where life is discovered. I feel that we push through our moments of deep breaths, agonizing sweat, unbearable pain, and willed endurance in search of our true character. We ask ourselves, Will my character be good enough when it counts the most? This true-life story is about the defining moment for men,

and how their choices defined another's. History is full of these moments. In fact this story is played out on the frozen canvas that killed so many in '96 [referring to the events recounted in Jon Krakauer's book *Into Thin Air*]. David curled up and froze near the summit. A high price to pay in search of internal value. I guess for me, it's all about who I take on the journey with me—my buddies, my wife, my God. They challenge me so that I may grow. I grow so that I may lead. I lead so that I may challenge. I challenge so others may help me find myself.

I wonder how many I have left to die of loneliness and neglect while pursuing my own mountaintop experience. To live like that is really a failure of vision. Because everyone God brings my way is, in small or large part, an important piece of my life story. On the way to the top, no one is discardable.

And friendships make even the toughest ascents possible. Mark summed it up nicely: "It's all about who I take on the journey with me."

Tuned In for Distress Signals

The Surfrider Foundation has created a thriving organization that helps protect the world's oceans and beaches through activism, conservation, and education. Are we talking about surfers doing this? Yup. You may be surprised, but surfers are some of the most passionate volunteers for the environment that you can find. Unless end times religiosity has clouded your thinking, you have to admit it is godly, biblical, and mission-critical that we help protect our environment.

And here is another thought: We need to extend that same passion and activism to protecting other people—in our communities, and around the world. We are created and called to connect to more than our own circle of friends. We're put on earth to care for and champion the human community as a whole, and the natural world we depend on.

To be truly connected to others means we notice, we care, and we're willing to pay the price of meaningful service.

A story illustrates my point. Everyone has heard about the *Titanic*, but few know about the *Carpathia*. She was the ship that pulled most of the freezing bodies from the icy Atlantic when the *Titanic* sank in 1912.

Interestingly, there were two other ships closer to the *Titanic* that evening. All three ships heard the distress signal, but only one steamed at full speed through the ice fields to rescue hundreds of survivors. The other two ships, the *California* and the *Birma*, took a more cautious route. Most specu-

TO BE TRULY CONNECTED TO OTHERS MEANS WE'RE WILLING TO PAY THE PRICE OF MEANINGFUL SERVICE.

late that they did not believe the first sets of distress signals from such an enormous and invincible ship as the *Titanic*.

When the *Carpathia* caught the distress signal just after 2 a.m., Captain Rostron turned his ship around and went at full speed to effect the rescue. With the help of lookouts he placed on deck, he dodged more than twenty exposed icebergs and countless submerged ones. On the way, he directed his crew and passengers to prepare rope ladders, slings, make-shift hospital rooms, and straw beds for survivors.

When they arrived at the debris field at 4:10 a.m., they shot flares into the night sky so that lifeboats could see their ship. Slowly, freezing men, women, and children began to surround the *Carpathia*. The ship's passengers gave up their comfortable state rooms and bunks to those who needed to recover from hypothermia.

Like the captain, crew, and passengers on board the *Carpathia*, I want to be a redemptive force in my community. I don't want to be so focused on my wishes and comforts that I completely miss the distress signals happening all around me. I want to be awake to the needs of people I meet in the course of an ordinary day who are going down for the count under the icy waters of depression, hunger, loneliness, drug addiction, or abuse.

Dr. Frank Blackmarr, a passenger on the *Carpathia*, was interviewed later about the causes of the accident. It was not so much the fault of the captain of the *Titanic* or the owners of the ship, he said. It was "speed and greed," he said, that sank the *Titanic*.

Locking In

A hundred years later, we are still surrounded by a world that promotes speed and greed as the all-American lifestyle.

What a lie! You and I are put here for a much larger adventure. It's about more than just us and our thrills or achievements, no matter how riveting they are. We're here on a mission we can't succeed at without meaningful friendships. And countless others won't succeed either—and may not even live through the night—if we don't clip in to their lives too.

Where could you and I start today to rethink things? We could choose friends and commit to families in ways that show them respect and invite them to be part of our adventure. We can slow down and listen, and make hard choices to come to the rescue when the distress signals sound.

We can lock in to people and to our world. Because we aren't created to be loners. We are made to connect.

Chapter
6

We Were Made to Fight

To fight is a radical instinct; if men have nothing else to fight over they will fight over words, fancies, or women, or they will fight because they dislike each other's looks, or because they have met walking in the opposite directions.
GEORGE SANTAYANA, SPANISH PHILOSOPHER,
ESSAYIST, AND NOVELIST

But you, O man of God...pursue righteousness, godliness, faith, love, gentleness. Fight the good fight of the faith.
1 TIMOTHY 6:11–12

Early in the morning of October 9, 1809, Captain Meriwether Lewis of the famed Lewis and Clark expedition took his own life and died a lonely man.

How could such an adventurer, such a noble champion for important causes, end his life only a few years after

becoming a national hero? Lewis had grown up in the out-
doors, hunting and fishing. He became an officer in the
Army and fought in numerous battles. When President
Jefferson wanted an expedition leader who knew Native
Americans and their languages, and could survive in hostile
circumstances, he picked his friend Meriwether Lewis.

But somewhere between the grand expedition of
1804–1806 and that lonely morning a few years later, something important had gone wrong.

What is known is that when he died, Lewis was deeply
in debt and addicted to alcohol. It is also known that these
problems didn't entrap him while on assignment for the
president.

Is it fair to conclude that as long as he was on a mission,
Lewis was able to keep other areas of his life in balance? I
think so. It seems to me that when he left adventure behind,
Captain Lewis left his passion for life behind too. I think he
just wasn't cut out for lectures, book tours, or pushing papers
as a government official with a desk and a routine.

The captain, maybe like yourself, was made for a more
dangerous life. He was made to identify something difficult—maybe even impossible—and then fight for it with all
his heart.

Risk takers and adventurers of all kinds share the same
DNA as Captain Lewis. When we put it to healthy use, we're
happy and productive; we can win a lot of battles. But when
we ignore our need to be part of a worthy, challenging mis-

sion, things can get off track in a hurry. We can end up losing the fight.

Of course, we live in a culture with pretty low expectations about what we're supposed to fight for. Take the popular Beastie Boys song with the line, "You gotta fight for your right to party!"[1]

Fight to party? Wow. Talk about a big idea for your life—that's just huge. Unfortunately, I can almost see that message displayed as a banner over every skate park and club I have been in. I do like a good party. But hedonism as the big idea for a life leads us to disaster.

Sometimes it seems that there's a conspiracy in our world to distract us from what really is worth fighting for. If we're not careful, we can find ourselves throwing all our waking hours into a campaign to win us the perfect body, the coolest car, the highest paying job, the most sexual encounters. But those aren't causes worth giving your life to, are they? We were created for something greater, a life calling where our gifts and passion and God's love for men and women can come together and be channeled toward a purpose that makes a long-lasting difference. A difference as sweeping and consuming in its own way as Lewis and Clark's mission to open up the West.

That's what I want us to think about in this chapter: What's worth dedicating your life passions to? What commitments are worth everything you've got?

In chapter 3, "The Miracle of Movement," we talked about

overcoming the negative influences in and around you, influences that fight against you, trying to convince you that change for the better just isn't possible. That's important because, in order to change, you have to believe that personal change is not just possible, but possible for you. And then you

WHAT COMMITMENTS
ARE WORTH EVERYTHING
YOU'VE GOT?

have to decide that you will do whatever it takes to invite positive change.

In this chapter I want you to think outside of your personal needs. I'm asking you to examine a

bigger picture, one that will reveal what you can and should do for others in need. So here we'll be asking the question, "What are you fighting for on behalf of others?"

A Hero in Our Own Time

In the book *Wild at Heart,*[2] John Eldredge points out that an underlying need of every man is this: He needs a battle to fight. Another way of looking at it is that every man needs to be a hero at something. (Many women, especially of the radical strain, are wired the same way.) But, unfortunately for a lot of us, our lives don't always support this need in healthy ways. Eldredge describes how spouses, parents, teachers, and even pastors can inoculate us, causing some of us to disregard this need to be a hero.

That book played a big role in opening my mind to the idea that maybe I was not broken after all, that I was perhaps created to love danger for a reason.

A radical person doesn't have to stuff the way he is made, or play it out in selfish, damaging ways. We can, for example, do some major damage for the cause of justice, righteousness, and honor. Think of the need for warriors in areas like fighting against poverty, drug abuse, pornography, corporate corruption, or environmental abuses. Jesus picked up a whip to chase scam artists out of the temple courtyard. So being somewhat tough or extreme can be helpful when we set out to change a system that is hurting the very people it is supposed to serve and protect.

Joan of Arc chose to fight as a teenager when she picked up her sword to lead a revolution against tyranny in 1429. Actually, people in her community had teased her for being a pious young girl who was too godly. But from childhood she'd had visions and dreams of a greater mission for her life, visions that warned her of the danger ahead and the immense importance for her to be both brave and devout. In the end, she stood against the armies of England, became a symbol of courage and freedom—and paid for it with her life.

In the same way Dietrich Bonhoeffer, a German theologian and pacifist during World War II, took action against the injustices toward Jews and other minorities. As an avowed pacifist when he was young, Bonhoeffer decided to change and participate in a plot to assassinate Hitler. Even though the effort failed and Bonhoeffer was imprisoned, he

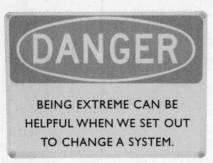

BEING EXTREME CAN BE HELPFUL WHEN WE SET OUT TO CHANGE A SYSTEM.

saw his role in the plot as his Christian duty. He was killed by guards in his cell only days before Germany was liberated by the Allies.

It takes a radical person to decide to stand up and fight. Every policeman who has been on the job for more than a few years has stories about coming face-to-face with evil. My good friend Mark, a Los Angeles County Sheriff's Deputy, told me about the first time he came face-to-face with a person who wanted to kill him. I will never forget his description of how he struck out first before he was struck down himself. It was frightening. The stories have one thing in common: In order to fight evil, officers must be willing to inflict measured damage in the cause of justice. Most cops sign up for the job because they like adventure (I come from a family of law enforcement officers). And most are not afraid of a good fight.

Of course, for most of us, our good fight is rarely physical. We do not carry a badge and gun, or need them. For us, our arenas of combat are predominantly spiritual, social, and relational. And, while the battle is no less important, it's likely to take place in and for our own families, communities, and world.

Fighting for the Family

Even if you're single, you'll probably agree with the statement that the human family is the strongest weapon for change known to man. I'd like to push that statement even further: *There is nothing more potent and able to impact the world today than a united family focused on the person and teachings of Jesus and called into serving their community.* Unfortunately, the very definition of family is under attack these days. Still, it's a fact of history supported by common sense and our intuition: Healthy, committed, moral families bring healing, hope, and life to their members, to their communities, and ultimately to their world.

You might be having a hard time, though, putting the words "radical" or "risk taker" with the word "family." Just doesn't work. Like putting bullfighting together with needlepoint, or racing at Talladega with reading sonnets by the lake. But trust me on this: I know radical moms and dads who are following Christ with reckless abandon and gracefully teaching their children to do the same.

What about you and me? Well, before we can do battle on foreign soil, we need to fight a more important battle at home. This is not the battle we fight against another family member but for our family members.

And for most of us, we need to start the fight inside ourselves. For example, why are we hiding our secret sins from the friends who could do the most to help us grow and change where we're weak? And what about the secrets we keep from our spouses—the ones who love us most and have the most to lose when we fall? Secrets keep us stuck. Deciding to fight dishonesty and pride in any area of private sin takes courage. It's a good fight that our generation needs to say yes to.

If you think you're wired for a big challenge on behalf of the family, commit yourself to eradicating pornography from

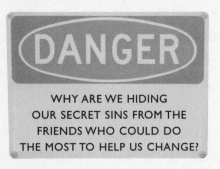

WHY ARE WE HIDING
OUR SECRET SINS FROM THE
FRIENDS WHO COULD DO
THE MOST TO HELP US CHANGE?

your computer, your hotel rooms, and your late-night movie watching. Those few minutes of adrenalized lust are devastating for us, and for the ones we've said we'd be loyal to. Someday that spirit of lust and degradation will find its way into the lives of our children and their children. Let's wake up and fight!

What about the twisted thinking of materialism that's an accepted part of the American Dream? The pursuit of material wealth has been "Christianized" in our western culture. One friend on his journey through the "Word of Faith/Name-it and Claim-it" movement decided that God wanted him to buy the Ford Excursion on faith, or rather, in his case, on credit.

Really?

Nothing wrong with a family wanting wealth—I hope to find some myself someday. But I don't see wealth as a

Christian right or as divine evidence of my upper-class faith. According to the writers of Proverbs and Ecclesiastes, wealth is usually a by-product of hard work and wisdom. Wealth can come to both the just and the unjust. When we don't think straight about money, we set up our families for financial mismanagement and debt.

Want to pick a good fight? Lead the way in teaching your kids to give more than receive, to view everything they have as on loan from God for a larger purpose (usually) than their own pleasure. Ask God for His view of what money is for in your family, and how you are called to steward it.

Another crippler of families—especially where there's a radical temperament around—is likely to be anger and out-of-control conflict. Why not take it upon yourself to fight for healthy, lasting peace in your family? You'll have to give up some adrenaline-fueled tantrums, and a few "rights," and maybe a "win" or two. I'm not talking about squashing all disagreements or choosing to be a terminal wimp. But Christ's followers are called to be peacemakers, not manipulators or people who know they can get their way if they get intimidating enough.

Fighting for the World

But our boundaries of concern and responsibility have to go much further than those issues that affect only those who are closest to us. Each of us is a citizen of other communities—

many of them, actually. Here are some of my other communities: neighborhood, church, Christian Surfers, business
network, state, nation, and world.

Talk about possibilities for getting in a good fight! Yet
most people who hang out in Christian circles for very long
realize that many followers of Jesus keep to a well-worn path
between home and church, and back again.

What kind of big idea for your life does that suggest?
What does it seem to say to others about God's heart for those
who are outside of church? Or outside of our comfort zone?

Interestingly, Jesus accomplished 80 percent of His ministry outside of a religious environment. In fact, the further
He got into his full-time ministry, the more time He spent in
the streets and the marketplace, at work, and in private
homes, and the less time He spent in the religious community. Of the twelve disciples he chose, none had "church"
credentials. Instead, they were a varied bunch of both blue
and white collar folks. Since He was God, Jesus certainly
could have pulled off His ministry on earth without anyone's
help. So why did He choose such ordinary men and women
to go out and change the
world in His name? May-
be to encourage you and
me that any ordinary per-
son could become a world
changer if God was in the
cause.

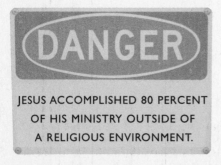

JESUS ACCOMPLISHED 80 PERCENT
OF HIS MINISTRY OUTSIDE OF
A RELIGIOUS ENVIRONMENT.

It's time you and I stepped off our well-worn paths and looked around for the opportunities for influence that God is bringing our way.

My oldest son, Joel, is living a radical Christian life at his public high school. In an environment of free sex and ubiquitous drug use, Joel maintains a vow of sexual purity and is publicly committed to following Jesus, and happy about it. And if you're wondering, he is "cool" by anyone's standards—good-looking, president of his class, and a good surfer. So I guess he experiences no shortage of female attention. Like myself, he will make his mistakes in due time. But today he has chosen to fight for his school, his friends, and his faith in an environment that thinks Christianity is a joke.

Bobby McDonnell has also chosen to fight. He married a beautiful, feisty El Salvadoran woman right out of college. At five foot ten, Bobby doesn't look like someone who would attack your cave and take your woman. But he is the kind of fighter people write books about. He is a scuba diver, entrepreneur, world traveler, and follower of Christ. And he has risked everything, and almost lost everything, in his fight to save children.

Love, in fact, is what got him into the fight. During his courtship and regular visits to his bride's home country, Bobby fell in love with the children who were left homeless and fighting for their survival on the mean streets of San Salvador. He has scooped starving kids off the streets while bullets flew through the air between corrupt government forces and corrupt rebel forces. He has fought to protect his new children from politicians and abusive relatives whose intentions were only to harm the already wounded.

Today, Bobby runs a ministry called Christian Children of the World. It provides food, schooling, and shelter for dozens of orphans. And Bobby doesn't just fight to give the kids a better today. He has a bigger win in mind: Ultimately, his mission is to raise children with the character and skills to be national leaders of the future.

Steve Bissel, another radical fighter, is fifty-three years old, holds a master's degree in electrical engineering from Stanford, and helps run a small but successful technology consulting company in the Pacific Northwest. How boring, right? Maybe not. Steve has taken his internal danger habit to a new level in the last few years by bringing the Jesus Film project into some of the most remote parts of Africa. He comes back from each trip with stories of danger, miracles, hardships—and incredible joy. In seven trips he has visited 160 villages and seen over ten thousand people choose to follow the teachings and person of Jesus.

Okay, there are downsides to his adventure. He has had an automatic rifle pointed at his head at late night road blocks. I asked him recently how much fear he has in those situations. Here is what he said:

The whole idea of voluntarily going and working in Nigeria, in what is one of the most dangerous parts of the world, with no human protection, is just plain crazy. Therefore, I am always extremely conscious of being 100 percent vulnerable, but at the same time 100 percent under God's protection. As a result, there is no fear at the time, just a strong assurance that what looks physical, like assault rifles in my face in the dark of night, is really just an embodiment of the spiritual battle that is raging. And in that case, I know that God has "got my back," and my job is to just push on and get the job done.[3]

I don't know about you, but I read Steve's words and I think, *Do I get that much thrill out of my extreme sport? And when I get to the end of my life, will I have that much to show for it?* How about you? I'm not saying dump what you love. I'm just posing a question: Are you and I channeling what we love—and the passion we bring to it—into the kind of challenge that can change lives forever, maybe even change our world?

Never Too Late for a Good Fight

As it turns out, the things we think keep us from living a radical life for God rarely add up to more than paper dragons. Things like our size, gender, personality, finances, family connections, bravery, athleticism, religious training, past failures, and even age—do we really think if we chose a battle with eternal payoffs that God could not find a way around those obstacles?

If you doubt me, consider the story of Caleb, one of history's most amazing warriors.

You see, Caleb was more than twenty battle-scarred years past retirement age when he got his big win—a family inheritance of land promised him many years earlier by Moses. He got the win because he was faithful and unafraid to simply believe the Lord. Joshua 14 describes how Caleb remained ready to fight all the way to eighty-five years old. In his own words:

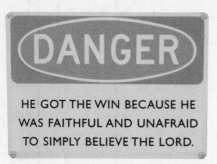

HE GOT THE WIN BECAUSE HE WAS FAITHFUL AND UNAFRAID TO SIMPLY BELIEVE THE LORD.

> Now then, just as the LORD promised, he has kept me alive for forty-five years since the time he said this to Moses, while Israel moved about in the desert. So here I am today, eighty-five years old! I am still as strong today as the day Moses sent me out; I'm just as vigorous to go out to battle now as I was then. (vv.10–11)

First, old man Caleb delivered his fiery speech to Moses. Then he went out into some of the most difficult terrain in the Promised Land and fought for what was his—and won.

I want that same passion and dedication to fight for God's agenda on this earth. And I want it right up to the moment they wheel me off to the nursing home. Actually, I want it past that. A friend of mine tells of the day he and his brothers wheeled his father through the doors of a convalescent center, knowing he'd never walk out. Their father was dying of cancer. It was one of those days that families just don't forget. But what my friend remembers first is what his dad said as they pushed his wheelchair through the doors.

It was a prayer: "Lord, bless me now on my last mission field."

That's the kind of warrior I want to be, right up to the end. I want to keep my life on mission, not wander off track and lose my taste for the dangerous life.

Let's take an inventory of the real battlefields in our family, community, and world. Let's thoughtfully and humbly ask God to show us the mountain or mission field that He is ready to give us.

Then let's go fight the good fight.

Chapter
7

Falling Down

There is no failure except in no longer trying.

ELBERT HUBBARD

While I know God refines us through trials, I'm not convinced
we absolutely have to go through smack-downs and tragedy
to be refined. I think it is more about surrendering
to God fully somewhere along the way.

JASON MENKE, REGIONAL COORDINATOR,
CHRISTIAN SURFERS UNITED STATES

Bind my wandering heart to Thee. Prone to wander, Lord, I feel it,
Prone to leave the God I love; Here's my heart,
O take and seal it, Seal it for Thy courts above.

FROM THE HYMN, "COME, THOU FOUNT OF EVERY BLESSING"
BY ROBERT ROBINSON, 1758

In the classic mountaineering book *Into Thin Air*, Jon Krakauer described his 1996 assault on Mount Everest. He concluded, "Climbing mountains will never be a safe, predictable, rule-bound enterprise. This is an activity that idealizes risk-taking; the sport's most celebrated figures have always been those who stick their necks out the farthest and manage to get away with it. Climbers, as a species, are simply not distinguished by an excess of prudence."[10]

I am not sure if surfers are smarter than climbers (I'm not smart enough to figure that out). But I am sure that every person with a danger habit likes the thrill of taking risks more than he or she likes the task of calculating the consequences. Those preferences sometimes lead to nasty results. The fact is, getting slammed is always in the cards for us.

That means that if you and I are serious about living on the edge of the cliff, we need to learn about falling off of it. And here I'm referring to the emotional and spiritual dimension more than the physical. (I hope you will agree that crashing on a mountain bike or kite board is less devastating to our long-term spiritual health than crashing morally.) Like a desert scorpion creeping into the house late at night, the things that we know will kill us will creep back into our half-fortified spiritual lives to harm us and those we love.

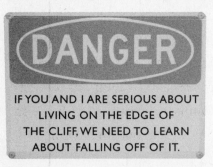

IF YOU AND I ARE SERIOUS ABOUT LIVING ON THE EDGE OF THE CLIFF, WE NEED TO LEARN ABOUT FALLING OFF OF IT.

What does failure look like? Well, the exact place or way that failure comes to each of us will vary, but any brotherhood of risk takers is likely to put together a familiar list:

- Failure looks like a deep physical, emotional, or moral injury that you think you can't survive.
- Failure looks like a discouraging "besetting sin" that feels deeply rooted into your life, no matter how hard you try to get rid of it.
- Failure sounds like someone you love crying on the other side of the locked door (and it's your fault).
- Failure makes you feel terminally stupid.
- Failure leaves you wondering how anyone—even God—could care about you and believe in your future.
- Failure usually costs you money, time, or good will.
- Failure leaves you wondering how to get back to where things were good.

Why is it that so many risk-oriented people find themselves living in such close proximity to failure? Maybe because that's where the hunt for the next thrill inevitably leads. I know many followers of Jesus who have been rendered mostly ineffective in ministry because their life is so full of personal damage that they can't outrun the hurt anymore.

In this chapter, I want to help you rethink failure. For one thing, God sees your failures differently (and more hopefully) than you do. For another, I can tell you from personal experience, no matter what has happened in your past, failure doesn't have to be a recurring pattern or career-ending injury.

With God's help we can learn to recover from failure, and—
even better—we can learn to prevent it.

The Top-Down View of Falling

Ever try to imagine how our failures look to God? Based on
my own experience and understanding of Scripture, I propose some thoughts for you to consider:

- He knows about all our failures, even before we've
  failed.
- He is waiting patiently for us to confess. He knows
  how healthy and cleansing confession is, and He
  desires it to come quickly and honestly. We're too
  proud to confess or admit it will probably happen
  again, but He knows it's our pride, not our failure,
  that is the biggest obstacle to recovery and change.
- Because of the work and redemption of Christ,
  God sees us as newborn members of His family.
  On the other hand, we think our failures prove
  we're born losers and outsiders.
- With God it is never too late to change (remember the thief who repented on the cross next to
  Jesus?). We think it's too late to change, but God
  knows we're only one prayer away from starting
  over.

There's a lot of good news here for risk takers! No failure needs to be final. We think we're a special case, too rotten even for God to rescue and change. But God is ready to step in—to rescue, to heal, and to redeem. So, for example, the next time I screw up, God won't be scratching His head and saying, "I sure didn't anticipate this problem. What am I going to do with Mike now?"

While God is saddened by our failures, they are not a mystery to Him. Imagine loving parents who really do know everything their troubled son or daughter does in secret and with friends. Yes, the parents know that some negative consequences of the child's foolish actions will never go away. And, yes, the sadness they feel is profound. But their love for the son or daughter remains unshaken.

Like a good parent, God is always at work to help us reach our best future. Sometimes natural consequences are the best teacher: Touch a hot kettle and your fingers burn. You learn to be careful around the stove. And sometimes God goes to work in our lives through people and circumstances to proactively help us to seize our full potential. The Bible word for this kind of personal training is discipline or chastening. Often it's our failures that provide the raw material for

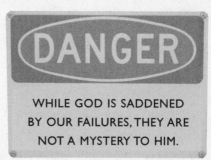

WHILE GOD IS SADDENED BY OUR FAILURES, THEY ARE NOT A MYSTERY TO HIM.

these training lessons. But we have to let God into our lives, or we'll waste the potential He sees in our losses.

Weaknesses of the Tribe

We've mentioned a number of areas where risk takers seem to crash most often. Here, I will address just two:

1. Rage. I still have daydreams of saving a beautiful woman from a madman in the Wal-Mart parking lot. In my imagination, I come flying into the mean dude's head with a wicked-looking elevated kick—or maybe a Chuck Norris spinning backfist to his temple. Yes, I would save the beautiful woman from her tormentor and restore her dignity. My battle wounds, of course, would be minor compared to the joy of yet another big win.

So far, I am happy to report this is only a daydream. No blood yet. I think my daydream is partly rooted in my love of a good fight, and partly—maybe mostly—because I get such a rush out of letting my anger loose.

Do you?

When I get angry, it is something powerful that boils up from my core. It promises to make right all my deeply seeded personal hurts and offenses. If I'm not careful, my rage can take over and destroy, not step in and rescue. Letting anger call the shots is costly. You've seen it. Anger makes good people say hurtful things, do hurtful things, things that felt right at the time but that they may regret for the rest of their lives.

Maybe that's why the Bible says, "A fool gives full vent to his anger, but a wise man keeps himself under control" (Proverbs 29:11).

Spiritually, when we let loose our rage, it's like someone pulls out the drain plug underneath our holding tank of peace—our God-given peace—and lets it all drain out. Jesus taught His followers to be careful who they give their peace to. In Matthew 10:13 and Luke 10:6, Jesus says (and I paraphrase): "If the person or home you are dealing with is worthy, let your peace rest on it. If not, let your peace return to you (and keep it to yourself)."

Every competitor and risk taker should consider how to gain and manage our own peace. Giving in to rage equals giving up your peace. And there just aren't many things in this world worth the trade.

Recently I was driving seventy miles per hour in the fast lane when a white jeep flew past me on the freeway and drove around me way too fast and way too close, all the while honking his horn at me and flipping me the bird. My blood boiled. But just before I hit the gas to run him off the road, I thought, Why should I give him my peace? I was listening to worship music in my car, and I was in a great place spiritually. I was enjoying the presence of God. Why throw it all away for one careless (idiotic) driver?

I decided in favor of my peace (and self-restraint). My choice behind the wheel that day was a significant victory for me, one I hope to repeat. I still struggle with dealing with anger in positive ways. I am ashamed to admit that I have used anger to try to gain control of situations or people. I am not talk-

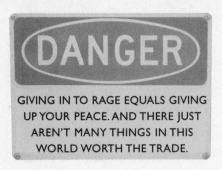

GIVING IN TO RAGE EQUALS GIVING UP YOUR PEACE. AND THERE JUST AREN'T MANY THINGS IN THIS WORLD WORTH THE TRADE.

ing about righteous anger (like taking on injustice in positive ways when no one else will). I am talking about one-of-the-seven-deadly-sins kind of anger.

It's easy for danger freaks to get casual about anger. We get it mixed up with testosterone or courage or being cool. But the first-century Christians took anger very seriously (and they had a lot more to get angry about than you or me). Paul told new Christians: "Get rid of all bitterness, rage and anger, brawling and slander, along with every form of malice" (Ephesians 4:31). The apostle James pleaded: "My dear brothers, take note of this: Everyone should be quick to listen, slow to speak and slow to become angry, for man's anger does not bring about the righteous life that God desires" (James 1:19–20).

The opposite of poisonous anger, according to Os Guinness in his book *Steering Through Chaos*, is the spiritual virtue of meekness. (Now there's a quality you don't hear much about in extreme sports!) Guinness eloquently describes how Jesus elevated the blessings of the meek and of peacemakers to a place of strength. He writes, "Whereas the sin of anger commonly stems from the feelings of inferiority and impotence, meekness stems from the accurate knowledge of one's strength. That strength, when submitted to God and thus under control, becomes true gentleness.... It can forego causing injury to others and instead work for peace and justice."[11]

So success on the issue of our rage problems comes down to a choice: Do we want the false strength of anger, or the world-changing power of meekness? Here's what Jesus promised: "Blessed are the meek, for they shall inherit the earth" (Matthew 5:5, NKJV).

2. Addictions. The journal *Nature Neuroscience* published a study in 2005 on the genetic characteristics of people who struggle with addictions. According to research done at the Rockefeller University Labratory of Biology of Addictive Diseases, there is a common genetic link between addicts and risk takers. No shock here, but people with impulsivity and risk-taking behavior are genetically similar to people who struggle with drug addiction.

Whether or not we are addicted to sex, alcohol, drugs, or cigarettes, all are often a by-product of a deeper pain. They can offer an escape from hurt or rejection (in our lives now or in our past). Unfortunately, many hold on to the addiction without ever dealing with the root causes. While medication and professional treatment are important and necessary, calling on God's healing power to bring a deep and dramatic healing is often the highest and best medicine.

I am not personally tempted to take drugs or embezzle money from the petty cash drawer. My struggle has always been with something more tactile. At various times in my life, sexual attractions have made things difficult in my thought life, not to mention my marriage and life of ministry. From the time I was a teenager I have tried to deal with this. Over time, I've realized I have to be more careful than the average guy about where I go, who I spend time with, and what movies I watch.

In the Bible, there is a remarkable story of something that happened to Jesus when he was invited to dinner at the home of a local religious figure. Look what happens next:

> When a sinful woman in that town found out that Jesus was there, she bought an expensive bottle of perfume. Then she came and stood behind Jesus. She cried and started washing his feet with her tears and drying them with her hair. The woman kissed his feet and poured the perfume on them. (Luke 7:37–38, CEV)

I read this story recently and began crying. I was in San Diego, California, on a business trip, surrounded by beautiful people all wearing beautiful clothes in a beautiful place. I had driven into San Diego the day before. It was a sunny seventy degrees with no wind and no humidity. I rented a convertible and drove onto Coronado Island for a series of business meetings. While driving across the Coronado Bridge I was listening to Aerosmith's song "Sweet Emotion" blast on the stereo.

Just a nice little head rush to get the day started.

At the Hotel del Coronado, right on the beach, there's not much to irritate a person, so how unusual to be overcome with God's presence while reading His Word in such a place. I was overwhelmed by the intensity of the situation described in the Scripture above, and I was struck by the two paths Jesus could have taken with this "sinful" woman.

Let's get something straight right now. If any woman starts washing my feet with her hair and her tears, I will be significantly challenged sexually. If she then pours expensive perfume on my feet, I can only imagine the mental and physical struggle. But Jesus came out of that situation sinless.

Even though we will never be sinless in this life, we do have the presence and power of Christ within us, to help us when we are tempted. And He really does help us when we ask. In my weakest moments, I have called out for His help and never been ignored. The apostle Paul talks plainly about a way of escape for tempted Christians in his first letter to the Corinthian church:

Don't be so naive and self-confident. You're not exempt. You could fall flat on your face as easily as anyone else. Forget about self-confidence; it's useless. Cultivate God-confidence. No test or temptation that comes your way is beyond the course of what others have had to face. All you need to remember is that God will never let you down; he'll never let you be pushed past your limit; he'll always be there to help you come through it. (1 Corinthians 10:12–13, THE MESSAGE)

Have you noticed the "safety exit" built into roller coaster rides at amusement parks? Right before you get on the ride there is always an escape door provided for people who are too frightened to take the ride. It is the same for us Christians, because the ride of sin we are tempted to take leads to death, but we can escape to life.

The next time you find yourself in the face of sexual or chemical temptation, remember to ask God to show you the way out. Just like the "safety exit" it will be there in plain sight. As someone once said, "We are the sum total of the yeses we say in life." Whatever you and I are saying yes to is defining who we are.

We can start saying yes to the exit more often.

Any "Freak" Can Make It

You and I are called, not to captivity to our failures, but to freedom in Christ. Not to the rush that comes from taking destructive risks, but to the wisdom that comes from above (which, James 3:17 says, "is first of all pure"). Jesus' disciples proved that God has a special place in His heart for freaks, outsiders, and danger addicts. But none of those labels means we aren't called and empowered to choose wisdom, meekness, and maturity as a new way of life.

Everything waiting for us from the very center of God's will, everything good and healthy and wonderful, is dependent on our ability to make good choices. And with God's help, we can. Whether it's making sure our energies are attached to a big and meaningful life passion, or choosing to serve others in fulfilling ways, or connecting in meaningful ways to family, accountability partners, and meaningful service, we can take the initiative to safeguard our lives before we find ourselves in a bloody mess at the bottom of the cliff.

In case it's helpful for you, I want to share two steps I've found consistently valuable in both preventing and overcoming failure.

First, throw off the weight of your besetting sin. In the book of Hebrews we read, "Let us lay aside every weight, and the sin which so easily besets us, and let us run with patience the race that is set before us" (Hebrews 12:1, KJV).

Everyone has "weight" in his or her life and everyone has a "besetting" sin. Weight is anything in your life that slows you down and keeps you from running the race God has given you. It's excess baggage. Imagine climbing a 5.14a with a small refrigerator strapped to your back, or paddling out into the surf while towing a half-sunk boat behind you. That is exactly how our besetting sins affect our mission.

One of my besetting sins is overcommitment. At one point in my life I was holding down a full-time technology sales job, teaching at church every Sunday, managing a local soccer team, serving as the president of the soccer club, overseeing the Christian

Surfers United States regional activities in the Northwest, and leading worship at Surfchurch. Where was I finding time for my wife and kids, much less for meditation and prayer? You can see the problem. I need to be accountable to my wife and family, and key advisers in my life, or I get in over my head.

You know what your besetting sins are. They've probably been nagging at your conscience for years. Now is the time to get help, confess your problem, make a plan. Now—before the weight makes you lose the race.

My second piece of advice: Build in "expansion joints." In his book *He-Motions*, T. D. Jakes shares a wonderful word picture about how concrete sidewalks are built. He points out that every good sidewalk has built-in "expansion joints" that allow the concrete to expand in the summer and contract in the cold winter. These expansion joints prevent cracking. He says most people have no expansion joints in their life and, with some failure, they

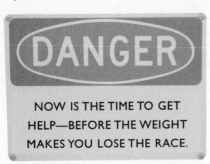

NOW IS THE TIME TO GET HELP—BEFORE THE WEIGHT MAKES YOU LOSE THE RACE.

crack and become useless. He masterfully explains how we need built-in grace (expansion joints) for ourselves, the kind that only comes from knowing Christ and the sacrifice He made for us.[12]

Practically, we build expansion joints into our lives by applying rules of grace for ourselves. Here are some to consider:

1. Be easy on others when they fail. Don't throw anyone under the bus when they really blow it. That is not only gracious and godly toward them but will come back to bless you and me someday when we blow it.

2. Understand how healing and gracious the Word of God really is. Read through the entire chapter of Psalm 119 and feel the power of God's love pour over your soul. Through the Bible the living, always-active Holy Spirit will minister deep healing to us when we fail.

3. Don't keep sin hidden. The former governor of New Jersey who fell from power after a secret homosexual affair was publicly revealed, wrote this profound statement in his recent book *The Confession*: "The closet starves a man and when he gorges it sickens him."[13] Secret sin destroys us faster than anything else you can imagine. It eats us up from the inside out. The process of confession, repentance, and forgiveness is critical for all of us who decide to take responsibility for our failings.

Picture This

In this chapter we've looked at two sides of the same coin:

- Risk takers and danger freaks seem to suffer from a higher failure rate than those who choose the safer route.

- Risk takers and danger freaks don't have to settle
  for failure as a way of life!

We can choose to preempt failure, we can choose to change, and with God's help, succeed.

It doesn't matter what the failure is or how many times we fall—we need to forgive ourselves, accept the natural consequences of our actions, ask God and those we have hurt to forgive us, stand up again, and begin walking forward with the Lord toward our life's mission. Sooner or later, we all fall down. But what matters most is what we do next. That's what sets rare radicals apart from ordinary radicals.

Redeemed failures wield a lot of power—I think a lot more than those who have never failed (assuming there might be one or two on the planet). Our life's mission is to bring good news of freedom to those who are chained in darkness, hopelessness, and sin. And our good news is summed up by the picture of the cross of Christ. Our stories are all the same, essentially:

What the cross of Christ means stands against everything this world sells to us. And at first, that big, fat, ugly cross seemed to block the path to our adventure. But once we realized we need its healing power every day of our life, that same cross turned beautiful and immensely compelling. The cross is the picture of our new beginning.

For those of us who know we are wrecked—those of us

who hurt others, those of us who can't seem to get it right—I tell you with all my heart that we desperately love the cross of Christ.

And for every other beat-up, discouraged, and discarded risk taker we meet, it's always the best true story we could ever share.

REDEEMED FAILURES WIELD A LOT OF POWER—A LOT MORE THAN THOSE WHO HAVE NEVER FAILED.

Chapter
8

Radically Realistic Expectations

"Your Father in heaven…makes His sun rise on the evil and on the good, and sends rain on the just and on the unjust."
JESUS, IN MATTHEW 5:45, NKJV

When the storm is over, there's nothing left of the wicked; good people, firm on their rock foundation, aren't even fazed.
PROVERBS 10:25, THE MESSAGE

One of the first American missionaries, Adoniram Judson, traveled to Burma in 1813 to bring news of Jesus to the Burmese people. It was six years before anyone in Burma believed what he was saying. Years later, his family was driven away from their home by war, and his wife, Ann, died in labor. Six months later, his new daughter died.

An article in *Christian History and Biography* magazine

describes the crisis of faith that followed for Judson: "The barbaric treatment he had endured [in Burma], the 'bitter heartrending anguish' of losing his beloved Ann, and the total destruction of his little church at Rangoon left Adoniram overcome with grief. For over a year he lived in a retreat in the woods, mourning his wife and child and struggling with his own past pride and ambition. He even dug his own grave and sat beside it, imagining how he would look lying in it. On the third anniversary of Ann's death, he wrote, 'God is to me the Great Unknown. I believe in Him, but I find Him not.'"[14]

Some travelers will get brutalized along this path of life and faith. In this chapter, I am not talking about what results from our own failures. I am talking about seemingly unavoidable trials that come at us from the outside, events that God doesn't seem interested in, or able to stop.

There is no hiding the fact that very bad things happen to very good people. When horror strikes and when God seems nowhere to be found, some are so disillusioned they leave the faith. And for every Christ follower who openly chucks it all, there are probably another fifty who follow the faith outwardly but inwardly they've all but checked out.

Bad things happen to everyone. And while bad things are equally hard on everyone, I've noticed that we radicals are quicker to walk out the door when major disappointments come. To me, that's just another version of staying stuck, of being just extreme enough of a person for the good times, but not for the bad. And I don't respect that quality in myself or others one bit.

When you and I arrive at our time of crisis, my prayer is that we break on through, and that God multiplies our blessings many times over after that.

FOR EVERY FOLLOWER WHO OPENLY CHUCKS IT ALL, ANOTHER FIFTY FOLLOW OUTWARDLY BUT INWARDLY THEY'VE ALL BUT CHECKED OUT.

Can we count on success, health, and happiness? I don't think so. I think it makes a lot more sense to seriously, prayerfully stare the ugly possibilities in the eyeballs, and do it now.

So I ask: What circumstance would cause you to walk away from your faith? Have you really thought that through? And are you prepared for life, people, and organizations letting you down?

Crash Test

Try to construct in your mind what circumstances in your life would cause you to stop believing that God is real or that God is good. What kind of crash test would make you so mad at God that you would tear up your ticket to the gates of heaven and walk away?

I have asked this question of a few close friends and their first reaction is to say something like, "Nothing would make me walk away. I might be mad at God, but I would never walk away."

Really? What about the death of a child, abandonment by your spouse, or sexual abuse by a pastor or priest? What if, because of unbearable events in your life or some chemical imbalance, you wake up one day and believe that God has permanently deserted you and probably never loved you anyway?

Heartbreaking tragedies happen every day in this world, and they cause many followers of the Way to quit the journey. Sometimes they're too angry to go on. Sometimes they're just tired.

Matt, a local surfer I know, used to be heavily involved in his faith and church on the North Shore of Hawaii. Just the other day Matt told me his story. His wife began having emotional experiences at their church with what she believed was the Holy Spirit. It seemed like a personal renewal for her and many others in the church. But even though he attended the same worship services, Matt didn't have the same experiences. He began to feel left out and somehow less spiritual than the rest of the crowd. His wife began spending more time with those she said were "closer to God than you." From there, things took a wrong turn. She had an affair with one of them and left Matt.

He is still angry at God and really doesn't know what to do about it. His answer so far is to steer clear of Christians and anything that smells like church.

Do you blame him? I don't.

I have been reading the life story of Brother Yun, who pioneered many house churches in China between the early 1980s and today. He now lives in exile in Germany with his family, but prior to that he was constantly on the run from the Chinese police, who to this day consider him a criminal.

What was his crime? Sharing with other people the gospel of Jesus Christ. Brother Yun is a born evangelist; in fact, he had brought two thousand people to faith in Christ before he turned seventeen years old!

For his "crime" he has been tortured by electrocution, beaten, kicked, defecated upon, and had nails shoved under his fingernails. While in prison he was tortured by the guards and the prisoners at the same time. But he never turned his back on his faith or his calling.

I have to wonder how I would have reacted in the same circumstances. I'm not saying you or I will be tortured for our faith. But we'll all suffer in this life. Unexpected things will happen that will threaten our faith, our emotions, and our relationships. If we don't think clearly about what to expect from life—and from God—we can end up angry, bitter, and far from Him.

In this chapter, we need to take a close look at what we expect from God, people, and organizations. It can make all the difference in how our life story ends up.

DANGER

IF WE DON'T THINK CLEARLY ABOUT WHAT TO EXPECT FROM LIFE—AND FROM GOD— WE CAN END UP ANGRY.

Radical and *Real*

There should be no downside to the battle, says the health-and-wealth crowd. But the Bible teaches us that our "best life now" comes specially wrapped in some major smackdowns. Think of the Mike Tyson scenario: Can you imagine Buster Douglas's corner man telling him to just focus on the positives? In the same way, can you imagine Jesus telling the imprisoned John the Baptist to claim his God-given right to blessings, health, and freedom?

Ridiculous!

Yet, there's a whole industry of sunshine pumpers on TV, in the pulpit, and in bookstores that dangerously oversells what we can expect from life and God. I occasionally meet well-meaning Christians who have swallowed the hyperfaith teachings, feathers and all. Don't buy it! It is appealing, but not real. It will set you up for huge disappointment and maybe a breakdown of your faith someday.

To be fair, part of expecting the unexpected is to admit that anything can happen. It is possible that God has an adventure more thrilling and wonderful than you can imagine. It's also possible that He will send you on a mission with your family…and your wife and newborn won't come back. At the beginning of a journey, you just don't know what lies ahead. Of course, the unexpected does not have to be negative. But applying Christian voodoo or magical words does not guarantee that it will always be positive either.

Mountaineers do not expect everything to go well. Tow-surfers wear life jackets and adventure racers carry radios. While they hope and pray for everything to go smooth, they expect things to go wrong—and plan for it. Similarly, our adventure with Christ will have its ups and downs. Does anyone really believe the best adventure can bring nothing dangerous, hard, or damaging? Then they're not on an adventure of faith anyway. They're on a spiritual bumper car ride.

The Bible tells us over and over that God is good, and what He does is good (see Psalm 119:68 as an example). But the world is not God. The world is its own thing—broken by sin and death, and besieged by Satan. Jesus told his disciples, "In this world you will have trouble" (John 16:33).

Illness, heartbreak, death—these are universal by-products of being mortals living "under the sun," as the writer of Ecclesiastes describes us. These tragedies are not in our control. They just happen.

They don't happen because God made them happen.

They don't happen because God doesn't love us. (And they don't not happen because God loves us middle-class white people more than the next guy.)

We are all "under the sun," and subject to the natural order of things.

So, can we have radical expectations for our journey with God that are also realistic expectations? I think so.

Here are some thoughts on what radically realistic expectations might look like for extreme followers of Christ:

- We can expect people and organizations to let us down. We shouldn't be shocked when people and organizations fail us. There's no perfect person, perfect company, perfect church. They're all made with imperfect people like us; some are trying to get

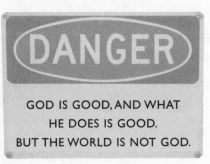

GOD IS GOOD, AND WHAT
HE DOES IS GOOD.
BUT THE WORLD IS NOT GOD.

  better, some aren't, and some are genuinely so wicked and corrupt we need to stay away from them. But reliable perfection isn't in the cards, even for well-intentioned, Spirit-filled Christ followers. When others let us down, it's not about God, it's about them.

- We can expect God to keep His Word and be true to His character. He is good, He is trustworthy, He is strong, He cares, and He is forever helpful to us along the way of danger. So when disappointments come, we can count on His goodness. Any temptation to blame God for evil in our lives is a lie straight from hell. The apostle James was aware of how much damage can come to the faith of Christ followers during trials. He wrote: "Do not be deceived, my beloved brethren. Every good gift and every perfect gift is from above, and comes down from the Father of lights, with whom there is no variation or shadow of turning" (James 1:16–17, NKJV).

- We can expect God to be always with us. Ask any Christ follower who's been through a divorce, a horrible illness, a family tragedy—God's tender presence is often the gift they remember most from these times. One of His names, after all, is "Immanuel," which means "God with us." And Jesus said, "I will never leave you nor forsake you" (Hebrews 13:5, NKJV).

- We can expect the human risks to go up as the danger quotient of our choices goes up. Say you feel called to bring aid by chopper to villages in the Andes, or bring health clinics to children in the jungles of Irian Jaya, West Papua. Then you can expect your risk of accident or illness to be quantifiably higher than for the Sunday school teacher who stays home in Peoria, Illinois. God will protect you, and provide for you, but the risk factors remain. You won't suddenly become immune to consequences because you're choosing to serve Jesus in dangerous places.

- We can expect to see God redeem things that are sad, tragic, and corrupted. Redemption—bringing life out of death—is what God loves and does best. His name is Redeemer, and if we let Him, we can expect Him to always be at work for our good in any situation, even the miserable and tragic ones. In fact, God is so committed to the act of redemption that He wants us to practice the same value in our own lives—He wants us to help bring restoration, reconciliation, and healing to injured lives and environments around us.

Preparing for the Journey Ahead

As I write this I am planning a climbing trip to Smith Rock in Central Oregon and a surf trip to Vancouver Island, Canada. My blood starts to race as I shoot off e-mails, invite others to join me, list items to take on the trips, MapQuest the directions, and calculate where the gas money will come from. For me, preparation is part of the thrill, and I love it.

In the same spirit, we should prepare for God's adventure, and in that spirit I suggest for serious Christ followers two key moves to make ahead of time:

1. Know Your Mission. Let's say at this point you put the book down, walk into the kitchen, and announce your intention to live your life for Christ as if it were really an adventure. Not just any adventure, mind you, because you've realized this is a God-given adventure designed just for you.

"I realize that it was never supposed to be easy," you proclaim, full of zeal. "I understand now that I have been created with a built-in wild streak because God wanted me to go do something wild with it—something for His kingdom." You're so pumped you can't wait to get started.

Then a more practical friend asks, "What is the adventure exactly? I mean, what will you actually do? Can you describe it for us?"

The answer to this very simple, mission critical question was already answered by Christ Himself: "Go into all the world and preach the gospel to every creature," He told his followers after the Resurrection (Mark 16:15, NKJV).

Our mission is simply to do the works of Christ and say the words of Christ. It doesn't matter if we are an elected official, professional snowboarder, evangelist, or boat salesman, out of our relationship with Christ Himself we should be doing His works and saying His words.

What Jesus told his followers to do at the end of His life on earth was actually an echo of what He'd already told them during his years of ministry. In Matthew chapter 10, we read about Jesus sending His disciples out as His representatives to teach and preach the gospel of His kingdom. His directions read like instructions for a road trip—how to travel, what to take, who to look for, who to watch out for, how to treat unfriendly strangers. But the key words are go and proclaim (vv. 5–27). And that is our mission too. Whatever our role in life, whatever our job, whatever our age, whatever our personality, we are to go on Christ's behalf and proclaim the message He came to proclaim.

To proclaim the gospel certainly doesn't mean we have to be rude and overbearing, or wear cheap suits and poofy

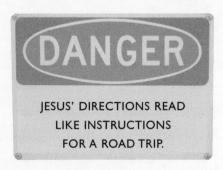

hair. Our message is Christ's, and the power for it to accomplish His will is God's. We proclaim the gospel by more than words too; we spread it by the way we work, pay our bills, make friends, and raise our kids.

JESUS' DIRECTIONS READ LIKE INSTRUCTIONS FOR A ROAD TRIP.

By going and proclaiming, we are sharing Jesus with those who don't know Him yet. In our broken world, in every opportunity that comes our way, we are His ambassadors, His stand-ins. In the margin of his Bible, John Wimber once wrote, "I must believe everything Jesus believed and I must do everything Jesus did."[15]

2. Count the Cost. You wouldn't climb Everest without a plan. You wouldn't buy a car or build a house without taking stock of your finances. In the same way, we need to calculate our readiness for the journey of faith in Christ. In a story one day, Jesus warned about the consequences of doing anything less:

Suppose one of you wants to build a tower. Will he not first sit down and estimate the cost to see if he has enough money to complete it? For if he lays the foundation and is not able to finish it, everyone who sees it will ridicule him, saying, 'This fellow began to build and was not able to finish'" (Luke 14:28–30).

Some reasonable Christians who have gone before us have fallen into adultery, rage, disappointment, or debt along the way. We shouldn't suppose that we're smarter or stronger or more spiritual then they. No doubt, we will also be tested along the way. And we need to be clear-headed about what we've signed up for.

Before Donna and I decided to move to the Oregon Coast to help pastor a church and work with Christian Surfers United States, we asked many questions about the issues and dangers facing pastors in the region. We kept hearing that in this area pastors must deal with pervasive issues of poverty, depression, and substance abuse. The Coast, though stunningly beautiful, suffers from higher unemployment and more rampant drug use than anywhere else in the state. There are higher ratios of unmarried couples living together, and divorce and separation are more common.

As you might expect, pastors and others in the helping professions must wade through all this wreckage. Many sojourners before us have paid a significant price to serve God in this area. Some churches have shut down while others only limp along, barely paying the bills.

I'm glad Donna and I thought about and prayed through these issues before we packed our first moving box. We counted the cost as best we could, then we both agreed the risk was worth the reward. For us, the calling to love surfers and serve their beach community as volunteer pastors was too great, too exciting, too necessary, and too critical to pass up.

The Best Place on Earth

Back to Adoniram Judson, the missionary we met at the opening of this chapter. Surely when Judson committed his life to spreading the gospel in a faraway land, he was hoping and dreaming for good things—for success, health, and happiness. Yet he and his family experienced heartbreak and death.

In spite of all he suffered, Judson didn't chuck his faith. His mission was clear, his heart was set, and he had counted the cost. With God's help, he broke through that time of terrible testing. In time...

- he recovered his health and spirit enough to translate the Bible into the Burmese language;
- he helped plant one hundred churches; and
- he led over eight thousand people to Christ.

One life, one commitment, and one surprising God. I believe that when we find ourselves doing what God has created and called us to do, we're in the right place—the very best place—no matter what challenges we must face.

Donna and I came to the Oregon Coast with our eyes and hearts wide open, and for my family the blessings have been beyond description. The fact that things will probably never get easy isn't lost on me. Plus, I'll make mistakes along the way. But we are where we're supposed to be, doing what we love, doing our level best to go and proclaim.

And for us, that means right here is the best place on earth.

Finishing Well

Sometimes the horror of losing my first wife to cancer still catches me and overcomes me. A violent sobbing rushes in and overtakes my body, my breathing, and my voice. It can catch me almost anywhere. I might be watching a movie or documentary about cancer or death. I can be in my car listening to a song. I could see someone walking down the street that looks like her. Whatever the circumstance, the memories of her last hours flood in, and the ghost of that pain becomes almost tangible. Probably those memories and that experience will stay with me for as long as I live.

In this last chapter of *The Danger Habit*, I want to share with you a very personal story of danger, risk, loss, death, and—yes—triumph. It is the story of what one radical champion for God can accomplish in the most painful circumstances. It is a story of extreme faith that continues to inspire me and others to make extreme choices. And my prayer is that it will do the same for you.

Heart of a Champion

I met Lisa Johnson from Crystal Lake, Illinois, when I was twenty-two and attending Judson College near Chicago. Ironically, the guy who was her fiancée at the time asked me to take her to a rock concert. He had the tickets, she wanted to go, but he had to work. So he called me, a trusted friend, to take her instead. I eagerly agreed to his plan, especially after noticing she was a sexy, tall blonde who loved to party.

A relationship developed. What can I say? We found we had a lot in common, including a passion for standing close to the edge in life, and some similarities in how we were bent and broken. A year later we were married and began our lives together. We were completely in love.

But after six years, we got some terrible news. Lisa was diagnosed with Hodgkin's disease, a form of cancer. We were living in Lancaster, California, by then, and had two small boys: Joshua was only a few months old, and Joel was three. And we were afraid. We were told, though, that if you have to have cancer, Hodgkin's disease was one of the better ones. With proper treatment, she had an 85 percent chance of beating it.

Over the next year and a half Lisa fought a brave battle that left her in tremendous pain. The chemotherapy and radical anticancer diets broke down her body. She lost all her hair and had two thick rubber tubes coming out of her chest (for the chemo to flow into her veins). But no matter how hard she fought, it became apparent that the disease was winning.

Yet while her body was being destroyed by a hidden enemy, her spirit was coming alive. In our church, and in Lancaster, she became an angel of faith and prayer for others during that time. She wrote to old friends from high school and told them about the wonders of Jesus. She would call people and pray with them for their needs, not her own.

I'm still inspired by her champion's heart. I am overwhelmed at how much she overcame just

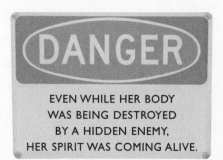

EVEN WHILE HER BODY
WAS BEING DESTROYED
BY A HIDDEN ENEMY,
HER SPIRIT WAS COMING ALIVE.

to keep her joyous glow and her ability to navigate through each painful day. Yes, she had moments of despair and grief, especially when thinking about leaving her family behind. But she never blamed anyone or became bitter.

Lisa loved to laugh, so small talk was okay, especially if it was funny or just lighthearted. But as her death approached, she wouldn't put up with visitors who complained or talked poorly about others. To Lisa, these kinds of conversations were a waste of time. On all levels—spiritually, relationally, emotionally—she wanted to know what was really going on with each person at her bedside. She had an amazing way of getting to the point, and she obviously felt an urgency to know each person who came to her room, and to know them deeply. She wrote long letters to her family too. She wrote in a separate journal for each of her young boys, and spent time buying them gifts for each of their future birthdays. She wrote in a journal just for me.

Even now, many years later, her example inspires me to pursue deeper friendships. I want to avoid conversations that are hurtful or a waste of time. What can make a mostly selfish man get a whole new perspective on life? Watching his lovely wife die while she remained focused on God's goodness and the people He brings her way—that'll do it.

Lisa was thirty when she died. At her funeral in July of 1995, many of the hundreds who were there had a new-found faith in Christ because of how Lisa finished her life on earth. At a large church near Chicago some time later, Lisa's closest friend and bridesmaid at our wedding, Christine Des Rochers, was baptized in the same dress she wore at Lisa's memorial serivce in honor of the influence Lisa had had on her faith. Christine is a pastor now for Willow Creek Community Church outside Chicago and remains a living testimony of Lisa's passion for Christ.

I'll admit it's easier for me to look back now and see the bigger picture, and Lisa's amazing example for us all. But at the time, it was different. I was in the middle of a battle for my wife's health. Honestly, I was fighting for my own sanity too.

I remember feeling confused, foolish, and very scared. I remember the look of confusion on Joel's face—and the awful feeling I had that I'd never be able to really explain what was happening. I remember how angry I felt to know that two-year-old Josh would never remember his mom. After she was gone, I remember how quickly I ran from grief into easy relationships and activities that helped kill my pain, but only temporarily.

I'll tell you this: In the midst of it all, none of it struck me as an "adventure" and my faith felt like it was hanging by a thread. With my wife in the next room with tubes coming out of her and poison flowing in, I just couldn't see our situation from an eternal perspective.

Many people who loved Lisa still feel the pain of loss and question why this happened. My own two sons have to live a lifetime with an empty place in their souls.

But I see things differently now. It's ironic, but now I can view our family's fight with cancer not as a detour that led to death, but as a death that led to so much life. Even though she died young, Lisa finished strong. She hadn't always been stable or sensible. She certainly wasn't perfect. But during her biggest test, she made choices that brought healing and new life to many.

Which leads me to pose one of the most important questions that's ever crossed my mind.

"How Can I Get More Out of My Death?"

More excitement. More energy. More success. Better relationships. Better sex. Better abs. People pay thousands of dollars for products and advice so they'll know how to get more out of life.

But I want to know, how can I get more out of my death? Lisa taught so many of us the importance of how we

WHEN ALL IS SAID AND DONE, WHAT AM I GOING TO LEAVE BEHIND THAT WILL REMAIN?

finish. When all is said and done, what am I going to leave behind that will remain? Jesus talks about His followers producing "fruit that remains." Everyone knows that natural fruit that we buy at the store doesn't remain. It spoils in a matter of days. But spiritual fruit, true fruit produced from a life of service and passion for Christ, will remain for eternity.

That's what I want to take to my death by the truckload.

Theodore Roosevelt once said, "A man should pay with his body for his beliefs." How badly do we really want to follow Christ? How committed to developing a fruitful life are we really?

And so I think one way to identify spiritual fruit in my life is to think about my own funeral. I know it sounds morbid, but stay with me for a moment. Over three thousand years ago Solomon wrote, "The mind of the wise is in the house of mourning" (Ecclesiastes 7:4, NASB), and he clearly wrote Ecclesiastes trying to answer the big questions of life with approaching death in mind.

Have you ever wondered who will be standing up at your memorial service to share how your life impacted theirs? Will anyone say their life would be somehow much less if you hadn't been their friend? How many will miss your presence and example in their lives? And what will you leave as an enduring legacy for your own children?

Okay, before you throw the book across the room, remember, I'm not suggesting that a life is measured by funeral attendance. A mother who quietly pours her life into her children may not have a big turnout at her memorial service, but think of her eternal joy when she sees her children come into their calling in life, and she finally sees the lasting results of her prayers and love and sleepless nights. She finished strong, and produced a fruit that will remain.

If we're honest we'd say that most people we know seem

to just stumble toward their futures, trying all the while to keep disaster from crashing down on them. They think if they can do that without breaking anything or anyone, they're a success.

But Lisa's example, and the example of many others, tells us something different and better.

Living for What Remains

In the previous chapter, I proposed that the way you and I make an impact on this world is to *go* and *proclaim*—doing the words and works of Christ in a way that honors Him. How, practically, do we do that?

I think we start with the passions, abilities, and opportunities God has given us. We start like the boy who brought Jesus his lunch of five loaves and two fishes. We bring ourselves to Him. What happens next is mostly up to Him.

This means that living for what remains will look different in many respects for me than it does for you. You may pour your energies into feeding the poor; I might pour my energies into teaching and preaching. You might mobilize ministries for the addicted, or work with others on the front lines fighting against genocide, poverty, and disease in Africa. I might run a company, or work in a warehouse. You may go on to be a sponsored athlete who brings light and hope to a confused and selfish world. I might…well, you get the picture.

Either way, when we invest the gift of God in lives (as a father or mother invests in their child), we change what happens in time and in eternity. That is fruit that lasts forever.

Which leads to an interesting outcome for humans, but especially for us extreme temperament types: The more radically we follow Jesus, the more our lives become about Him, and the less they become about us. To pour our life into things that remain, into fruit that remains, we have to let go of our need to be the center of attention, the subject of our own life story.

DANGER

WHEN WE INVEST THE GIFT OF GOD IN LIVES, WE CHANGE WHAT HAPPENS IN TIME AND IN ETERNITY.

This is what Jesus asked His disciples to do. "Take up [your] cross [die to self] and follow me," He said. Then He took His message to even greater extremes. We could paraphrase and expand the Great Commission like this:

> "Go into all the world [take ridiculous risks in every possible place on earth if needed] and preach the gospel [talk to everyone, not about you, but about God's redeeming love—and don't be a self-righteous jerk about it]." (Mark 16:15, NKJV)

Lisa accomplished this mission under extreme circumstances. Did you see it as I was retelling the account of her death? Living under the sentence of death, she thought mostly of others, provided mostly for others, listened and prayed mostly for others. People came to her room to bring God's comfort, but she was the one who usually gave it to them. She decided that to make her life remain—to see it morph into something greater and eternal—her story couldn't be just hers. It had to be the real story happening on this earth—the story of God and His great love.

There's one sticking point about living the kind of life we're talking about here. A big one for go-anywhere, do-anything risk addicts. As counterintuitive as it sounds, the life we've been wired to live from day one is too much for us. In fact, without a huge infusion of God's presence and power, we'll quickly crash. We don't need more and better of us. We need more of God.

Which brings me to a word you won't usually hear rolling off the tongue of your average extreme athlete.

Epiphany

Since the first century, the church has celebrated a holiday called Epiphany. It falls on the calendar around the winter solstice—the day when the days stop getting shorter and darker, and start getting longer and lighter. The term *epiphany* comes from a Greek word meaning "manifestation" or "appearance." When someone tells you they had an epiphany about something, they mean that they experienced a sudden insight or illumination. It's like someone turned the lights on for them. An epiphany moves you from darkness to light.

Spiritually, an epiphany can only come from God. What we bring to it is need, darkness, hopelessness without God's help, and a desperate desire for more of Him. More of His presence. More of His light. The apostle John wrote: "This is the message we have heard from Him and announce to you, that God is Light and in Him there is no darkness at all" (1 John 1:5, NASB).

To get anywhere at all on our mission as His high test followers, we need more of God. Much more. What we need is an epiphany.

True epiphanies are deeply personal and rare. Ask your friends something like the following question: "Tell me when you have seen or felt God pour completely over your life and your soul? When did He speak profound truth into the deepest parts of your mind? When was that exactly?"

If such a thing has never happened to them, they'll shrug. Maybe they'll think you've lost your mind. But if it has happened, they'll want to tell you, even if they struggle to put the experience into words. It is a defining moment for them. Everything that has come afterward depends on it.

True epiphanies never happen on our timeline. We can't slot one on our calendar. Don't think, Somewhere between the kids' soccer game and the last episode of *Lost*, I plan to have the epiphany Mike is talking about.

Not gonna happen.

If you have truly fallen in love with someone, you know exactly what I am talking about. Did you plan it out? Did you orchestrate the order of events that led to the overwhelming experience of falling in love? No. It came crashing in on you completely unannounced, and you were unprepared to deal with its power over your life and emotions and thoughts and dreams. It consumed every moment of your day. You began to see everything in a different way, because your heart was now captured and filled by someone else.

So how and when does an epiphany happen? Often, God brings His healing light at the end of tremendous pain or the midst of some deep anxiety or storm in life. For example:

- St Francis of Assisi had his epiphany on the eve before his first real hand-to-hand combat as a young soldier in the French countryside.
- Jacob had his on the night before meeting his estranged brother Esau, who he thought would try to kill him the next day. (Genesis 32:24–29)
- Moses had his while on the run from his Egyptian royal family. (Exodus 3)
- The apostle Stephen had his moments before he would be stoned to death for his belief in Christ. (Acts 7:55–56)
- A local surfer had his after being chomped on the leg by a great white shark.

- A young mother had hers when her husband took off to live his own life, leaving her with three kids and no way to pay the bills.

A friend of mine always says that God shows up at 11:59 but is never late. My epiphany happened during my first week of college. I was surrounded by people and places I did not know or like. I was two thousand miles away from the Southern California beaches and lifestyle that I loved so much. I was twenty years old, desperately lonely, and angry at the world. I was walking down a sidewalk one evening when I heard singing coming from the campus chapel. Out of curiosity I entered and slipped into the back row.

I had walked into a prayer meeting. Sitting there in the back, I bowed my head and started to pray by myself. I was desperate. For the first time in my rebellious, self-centered, no-unacceptable-risks life, I felt that I had come to an end of trying.

Finally, I quit.

As others began to speak out in prayer, I felt a warm, thick something pour down over my entire body. It was like someone

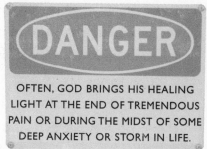

OFTEN, GOD BRINGS HIS HEALING LIGHT AT THE END OF TREMENDOUS PAIN OR DURING THE MIDST OF SOME DEEP ANXIETY OR STORM IN LIFE.

was pouring warm cooking oil over my head. This powerful presence began to heat and heal my insides. I started to cry.

Through the tears I began to ask God to forgive me for the times I had mocked Him, the times where I hurt others. I began to remember terrible things I'd done that had been pushed out of my memory. The Spirit of God was leading me to Himself, but leading me first on the path of remembering and confessing and, finally, forgiveness.

Nobody asked me to walk to the front or sign a membership card. Nobody prayed for me, and I don't even remember anyone else talking to me. What happened, happened inside me, and in solitude. It was a radical God rescuing a radically lost young surfer who was on the brink of making an even worse mess of his life.

God shone His light into my darkness on that cold night. That epiphany marked the beginning of change and healing in my life that, thankfully, is still going on. And it is the single most significant moment for me.

The Starting Point

If it hasn't already happened, God can one day fill you with His presence and power. You will know then that He has been pursuing you your whole life.

My encouragement to you is to stumble in out of the cold and dark, sit down quietly in His presence, and do the one thing that those in the fellowship of danger addicts swear we'll never do—quit.

This is your new starting point. This is the beginning of

the real race of your life. This is the place where God always waits for you, even if all you see are years of wasteful, idiotic, destructive trying.

In case you need help getting the words out, I've suggested a few below. Say them from the middle of your crazy heart.

Only God knows what will happen next.

"I Quit"

Lord, forgive me for living a remarkably selfish life.
I quit.
Against all odds I want to serve You alone.
I know that You created me to be a risk taker
for a reason.
Lord, use my extreme nature for Your kingdom,
only for Your kingdom,
whatever the cost.
I want to tell Your story now, not mine.
Teach me to serve other people without regard
for myself.
Teach me to give. Teach me to love.
Teach me to be a disciple
who brings Your words and actions to others
wherever I go.
Amen.

Acknowledgments

To all the locals who let me surf spots they broke into many years before I showed up, thanks for sharing the waves. To the CSO gang like Stan Michelson, Jason Menke, Big Glen, Buzzy, Mike Jipp, The Goldens, Mike and Tiffany, and Drew and Sarah for starting with us and staying around for the long haul. To Jeremy "Snapper" Rasmussen for coaching me into more barrels, and Rob Russo for making me such excellent surfboards. I would like to thank Peter Barton and Susan Russo for really honest feedback on this book's earliest version. To my friend David "DR" Rowe for pulling me out of the office and back to surfing. You had no idea then what changes God would bring through your simple act of friendship. My greatest appreciation goes to Jason and Stan for your close and lasting friendships and faithfulness to our ministry. I love serving with you guys.

I am forever grateful to the SEM guys for over ten years of loyalty, trust, and confidentiality. I still value Vic Anfuso's mentoring and Doug Crane's smackdowns. To the Wild at Heart small group, Tim, Doug, Ryan, and Jerry, for allowing such a deep, life-changing experience to happen in our lives.

To Jason Myhre and David Kopp at Multnomah Publishers for inspiring me to write this book—then teaching me how to write it. Judson College for its leadership in the world. My thanks to Mark Cripe and the Edge Foundation for the passion poured into this topic and the resulting study guides and blogs.

To my church family at Coast Vineyard Church in Lincoln City. You are all so loving and a shining example of what I always thought church should have been in the first place.

To my extended family—the Barretts, Johnsons, McBains, and the Ness clans—thanks for the ongoing love; especially to Mom and Dad, Joel, Josh, Caleb, and Ellie for the constant love. To my late grandmother, Ethel Barrett, who gave me a love for writing, storytelling, and an even deeper love for God. You were a great example to me.

My wife Donna deserves the highest plaudits for her undying support for and encouragement of this mission. My kids remind me this book never would have happened without her...they are so right! In this world Mothers usually do all the messy work and get none of the credit. In this case, Donna did all the unseen work and gets all the credit.

About the Author

M ike Barrett is a full-time executive with a global technology company and the volunteer teaching pastor at Coast Vineyard Christian Fellowship on the Oregon Coast. A graduate of Judson Christian College in Elgin, Illinois, Barrett went on to pursue some postgraduate work in theology at Fuller Seminary in Pasadena, California. He didn't finish that. But at the same time his career in sales and marketing began to rise. Prior to his current executive role in IT consulting, he was a corporate vice president for two publicly traded staffing companies and founder and CEO of his own technology consulting business.

Barrett returned to his passions of surfing and rock climbing in 2001, following a string of personal tragedies including the loss of his first wife Lisa to cancer and the failure of his business during the dot-com economic downturn.

Barrett's love for surfing not only aided in his personal healing process, but prompted him to eventually reach out to the increasing number of surfers in Oregon and the surrounding areas by founding Christian Surfers of Oregon, a loosely held organization of nearly five hundred surfers throughout Oregon and Southwest Washington. Today, he serves as a board member for Christian Surfers United States (www.christiansurfers.com), where he advises CSUS in the areas of chapter growth and leadership development.

At a young age, his grandmother, the late Ethel Barrett (an award-winning storyteller and author) instilled within him a love for storytelling. He now uses that talent to inspire change in the lives of radically minded people everywhere.

Mike Barrett makes his home in Lincoln City, Oregon, with his wife, Donna, and their four children.

Mike welcomes input from extreme athletes, bloggers, and radicals everywhere. Visit **www.dangerhabit.com** to join the conversation.

Endnotes

1. Paul Roberts, "Risk," *Psychology Today*, Nov/Dec94, Vol. 27 Issue 6, 50.
2. Thomas L. Friedman, *The World Is Flat*, (New York, New York: Farrar, Strans, Giroux, 2005).
3. John Eldredge, *Wild at Heart* (Nashville, TN: Thomas Nelson, Inc., 2001).
4. Brennan Manning, *The Ragamuffin Gospel*, (Sisters, OR: Multnomah, 2005), 78.
5. *Zondervan Bible Dictionary*, (Grand Rapids, MI: Zondervan), 748.
6. Dr. Frank Blackmarr, "The Titanic," available from http://www.encyclopedia-titanica.org/item/1145.
7. Lyrics are from *Licensed to Ill*, "Fight for Your Right," music and words by Beastie Boys, Def Jam Music/Brooklyn Dust, 1986.
8. John Eldredge, *Wild at Heart* (Nashville, TN: Thomas Nelson, Inc., 2001).
9. For documentation about Steve's ministry adventures, visit his website at http://www.izereproject.org.
10. Jon Krakauer, *Into Thin Air* (New York, New York: Anchor Books, 1997), 291.
11. Os Guinness, *Steering Through Chaos* (Colorado Springs, Colorado: NavPress Publishing Group, 2000), 137.
12. T. D. Jakes, *He-Motions: Even Strong Men Struggle* (New York, New York: G.P. Putman's Sons, 2004), 14–16.
13. James E. McGreevy, *The Confession* (New York, New York: HarperCollins, 2006).
14. Richard V. Pierard, "The Man Who Gave the Bible to the Burmese," *Christian History and Biography*, Spring 2006 Issue 90, 20.
15. John Wimber, *The Way In Is the Way On* (Ampelon Publishing), 204.

A uthor's note: If you're like me, you need to talk something through before you feel that you've fully experienced it. That goes for what you read as well as what you do. With that in mind, I offer this chapter-by-chapter study guide. It's meant to be used as a think or conversation starter for individuals or groups. And please don't let my questions limit where your imagination goes. Ask God to direct you in ways that will be most helpful to you personally. Use the "Field Notes" section at the end of each chapter entry for recording your thoughts and questions, or to write out a prayer. For study guides available for download, go to **www.dangerhabit.com**. Blessings on your journey!

—Mike

01. The Danger Habit

Mike tells his story of growing up addicted to thrills, and how a passion for danger and excitement has brought him some of the best memories of his life—and some of the worst. He casts a wide invitation to those who don't want to settle for ordinary but are ready to think in fresh ways about what it means to love living on the edge, an edge that Mike suggests may be very close to the true meaning of living by faith.

1. What is your danger habit? Describe your most thrilling moments of risk-taking in pursuit of it.

   _____

   _____

   _____

2. Mike writes, "Living on the edge makes life more exciting, especially for people who need to escape." Is the need to escape a significant dynamic in your life? If so, talk about how that need shows up for you, and how you tend to respond.

   _____

   _____

   _____

3. For some, a danger habit leaves them feeling like an outsider—different, difficult, maybe dangerous. For others, it decides how they play, where they work, who they marry, who they hang out with. Talk about how your "habit of risk taking" has shaped your life.

   _____

   _____

   _____

4. Mike writes about how a drive for thrills can also lead to pain in your personal life—your own or for those close to you. How about for you?

   _____

   _____

   _____

5. Have you ever connected your love of risk with the "big idea" of living by faith, or the thought that God might want you to invest your danger habit in something

unique and important for Him? If so, what insights could you share? If not, how open are you to exploring in this direction with Mike?

_____

_____

_____

DH Field Notes:

_____

_____

_____

02. A Profile of Opposites

Could any two people be more different? One gets as close to the edge as possible, the other stays far away. One makes a life-changing decision in minutes, the other processes options and ramifications for days, maybe years. One actually likes a little financial chaos, the other spends hours stacking and counting the family nickels. Mike describes two common opposite personality types: a radical temperament and a foundational temperament. Each has its own amazing strengths, and each a few big weaknesses too. Can two people with such differences coexist? Actually, says Mike, God made us different for an important and promising reason.

1. Which core statement do you most identify with:

   a. "Bring me a good feeling that I can depend on. That is when I feel happy."

   b. "Bring me something or someone dependable and logical. That is when I feel happy."

2. If there was a scale of one to ten, ten being most radical, where would you fall?

   _____

   _____

   _____

3. If you are more foundational, what have you learned from the radical people in your life? What are the areas where you experience the most frustration or misunderstandings with them?

   _____

   _____

   _____

4. If you are radical, what have you learned from the foundational people in your life? What are the areas where you experience the most frustration or misunderstandings with them?

   _____

   _____

   _____

5. Mike makes two important points in this chapter: God made you either foundational or radical for a reason (you're not a mistake); and God intends for you to move toward positive change (maybe with a person or people who are your opposite tempermentally). Do you agree with both points? If so, does the second point make you feel uncomfortable? Talk about it.

   _____

   _____

   _____

DH Field Notes:

_____

_____

_____

03. The Miracle of Movement

It's one thing to say we're risk takers by nature, and another to say, "God made me that way for a purpose." But even that's not the end of it. God also made us to want and need change. We don't have to stay stuck. Maturity means we wrestle with our unique strengths and our besetting weaknesses, but it also means we set out on a journey. We put our lives in motion. It's a commitment that too few radical or extreme people seem to choose, and the losses to them and those they love are huge. But it doesn't have to be that way. Personal movement toward a higher, rarer kind of radical is possible for anyone, and invites a God-sized miracle in our lives.

1. During what season of your life, or as a result of what event, did you change the most as a person? What factors then would you say put you in motion?

_____

_____

_____

2. Most of us feel at times that change, at least for us, is near to impossible. No matter how hard we try, we keep falling back into the same ruts. Do you identify with this scenario? Talk about where you are in your life—in motion or in a rut—and why.

_____

_____

_____

3. Who do you know who has seemed to change the most dramatically for the good? Talk about their before and after profiles. In your opinion, what was it that actually made change happen for this person?

   _____

   _____

   _____

4. Mike points to the biblical story of Samson as a tragic example of a gifted person who was unable to temper his danger habit, and unwilling to change. So, flip side of question number three: What "Samson" do you know (maybe it's you) who has never seemed to be able to change for the good? What negative consequences for the person and others around him or her can you identify? In your opinion, why has change not happened?

   _____

   _____

   _____

5. In regards to successful extreme living, what have you learned from watching the life of others in your sport or line of work?

   _____

   _____

   _____

6. Mike writes: "With God's relentless pursuit of my heart and mind, a few necessary miracles, and a lot of prayer, I know that I am moving slowly and purposefully toward the freed radical zone. It's what I want for my own life, and what I pray for yours." What would

you say to Mike about where you are now in terms of being in motion toward the "freed radical zone."

_____

_____

_____

DH Field Notes:

_____

_____

_____

04. It's Called "Adventure Faith"

Every radical person is hardwired for adventure. You dream about ice climbing, circumnavigating the globe in a catamaran, kayaking over sixty-foot waterfalls…whatever. But Mike says there's a bigger idea for your life, and a greater adventure waiting. It is what he calls "adventure faith." Adventure faith means you dare to consider that at the heart of your crazy passion is also a life-long adventure with God, and maybe the key to a life of influence and significance (something you figured adrenaline junkies like you would never qualify for).

1. Would you have signed up to ride for the Pony Express? If so, why: the danger, the outdoors, the speed, or some other reason? If not, why? Is there some other big adventure that you've sometimes dreamed about but not (so far) attempted?

   _____

   _____

   _____

2. Mike tells about how, after trying unsuccessfully to make a future happen by sheer energy and willpower, a friend came to him and said he was "like 'three yards and a cloud of dust,' meaning that I had a lot of flash at first only to fizzle out after a few yards." Do you recognize yourself in that description? How many plans have you made to serve God in some way, only to see them fail? Talk about it

_____

_____

_____

3. For people who are goers and doers, waiting on God (actually trusting that He will act) is really stressful. What about for you? Have you ever tried a "nonactive" spiritual discipline like fasting or silence before God? For how long? What was the result?

_____

_____

_____

4. Find a quiet place where you can be alone. Sit prayerfully but silently for three to five minutes. Just focus on God, His throne, and His glory. Then describe your experience in writing.

_____

_____

_____

5. How would you respond to Mike's question: "As you think back over your story—the spiritual and emotional journey that has brought you to this page—would you say you have opened yourself to the possibility of a life adventure with God?"

_____

_____

_____

DH Field Notes:

_____

_____

_____

05. We Were Made to Connect

Freedom and independence are intoxicating for radical temperaments. But the problem with the loner life is that some things come
hard or late or both. Important things, like genuine intimacy, for
example. Radical people seem to suffer from serial failure in the
relationships that matter most, relationships like a business partnership, a marriage, a family, or a church. And then there's the
mysterious challenge of achieving spiritual intimacy with God. But
Mike shows that we don't have to settle for less if we're willing to
lay aside some bad habits and old assumptions, take the time to
care and listen, and dump a lot of pride and self.

1. Looking at your life now, would you say you have
   a] many acquaintances but few or no deep friendships,
   b] few acquaintances and few or no deep friendships,
   or c] both many acquaintances and many deep friendships? What in this area would you change if you could?

   _____

   _____

   _____

2. Describe your most important friendship today, why it
   works, and why it is so important to you.

   _____

   _____

   _____

3. Would you agree with Mike's premise that radical temperaments tend to value personal freedom and independence above community connection and community responsibility? Why or why not?

_____

_____

_____

4. Are you seeing any changes in how you value independence versus relational connections as you age? If so, describe.

_____

_____

_____

5. How would you describe your past church experience, if any? Write down some qualities you would like to find in your ideal church.

_____

_____

_____

6. Are you comfortable with the thought that you were made for meaningful service? If you could do anything you wanted, what kind of service would you most want to provide your world?

_____

_____

_____

DH Field Notes:

_____

_____

_____

06. We Were Made to Fight

What's a contest without an opponent? Maybe that's why radical people are drawn toward, not away from, conflict. Of course, this dynamic can make for a ton of trouble—whether in a marriage relationship, on the job, or among friends. But Mike wants you to see that your scrappy, take-on-all-comers attitude isn't a genetic defect, and you don't need to leave it at the door. Like your other tendencies, it can help you rise to something more important than a fist fight. You can be a champion for people and communities and causes where others would just as soon stay safely inside. You just have to choose the right fights, know your real enemy, and then fight for the real wins.

1. If you would say you have a well-developed fight reflex, how has that shown itself in your past? How does it affect your activities or relationships now?

   _____

   _____

   _____

2. Would you say you're more comfortable fighting for something good or against something bad?

   _____

   _____

   _____

3. Describe the connection between your fight reflex and any of these situations that seem to apply in your life:

   - frustration
   - boredom
   - a perceived injustice
   - fear
   - disrespect
   - feeling like the underdog
   - shame
   - an exciting challenge
   - other

   _____

   _____

   _____

4. If you're married, would you say you throw most of your energies toward fighting with your spouse or for your spouse? Hint: This is a deeper question than you might think.

_____

_____

_____

5. What is going on inside your family that could be calling you to fight in positive ways?

_____

_____

_____

6. What is going on in your community that could be calling you to fight in positive ways? What about your world?

_____

_____

_____

DH Field Notes:

_____

_____

_____

07. Falling Down

Why is it that so many risk-oriented people find themselves stuck in addictions and destructive lifestyles? Maybe because that's where the hunt for the next thrill, the ultimate escape inevitably leads. In this chapter, Mike talks honestly about failure, discouragement, and living in bondage, and what it takes to begin to turn things around. Because you were created and chosen for freedom, not captivity and death.

1. What would you say has been the biggest failure in your life so far? What were the circumstances in your life at the time? To what degree would you say your danger habit played into that failure? How well would you say you have moved on from that experience?

   _____

   _____

   _____

2. One of Mike's definitions for failure is: "Failure sounds like someone you love crying on the other side of the locked door (and it's your fault)." Do you resonate for personal reasons with that scenario? If so, try to describe your experience in terms of a] cost to others, b] how you felt about it then, c] how you feel about it now, and d] how you hope you've changed since.

   _____

   _____

   _____

3. Do you notice seasons or cycles of failures in your life, or areas where you tend to fail over and over again? To what degree would you say these patterns define how you think and feel about yourself (not at all, a little, quite a lot, totally)?

   _____

   _____

   _____

4. Does the thought of getting back up again and starting over depress you or inspire you?

_____

_____

_____

5. In your areas of personal weakness and sin, what do you sense God was trying to tell you as you read this chapter? What is your response? Write it down as a commitment or a prayer.

_____

_____

_____

6. Mike writes: "Redeemed failures wield a lot of power— I think a lot more than those who have never failed." Have your wins and losses in those areas of weakness provided opportunities for you to help others? If so, how?

_____

_____

_____

DH Field Notes:

_____

_____

_____

08. Radically Realistic Expectations

What does it take to keep going down the road of adventure faith when people and institutions let you down (as they will)? Radicals tend to just walk out the door when things turn sour. But that's ultimately just another version of staying stuck. Mike helps extreme people reimagine long-term healthy attitudes and responses that will have made all the difference when we get to the final curtain.

1. Writes Mike, "While bad things are equally hard on everyone, I've noticed that we radicals are quicker to walk out the door when major disappointments come." Do you agree or disagree? Why?

   _____

   _____

   _____

2. Thinking back over your employment history and relationship history, how would you say you have reacted when people, organizations, or circumstances don't meet up with your expectations?

   _____

   _____

   _____

3. What has your church been teaching you about prosperity, health, and the promises of God? Do you agree or disagree with Mike's view that what he calls "hyperfaith" teachings set us up for disillusionment? Why?

   _____

   _____

   _____

4. Being as honest as possible, write down a worst-case scenario (or several) for your own life—the events that would most likely tempt you to walk away from your faith in Christ. Why would these trials be so hard on you? What does that tell you about what's important to you? Are your expectations mature and realistic?

   _____

   _____

   _____

5. Does someone in your life or in recent history come to mind who has had their plans changed by tragedy? How did they handle it? How did their response affect you emotionally and spiritually?

    _____

    _____

    _____

6. Would you say you have counted the cost of what it will take to faithfully follow Jesus for your whole life? If not, what might be keeping you from that kind of courageous, clear-minded assessment? If so, take a few minutes to write out in simple language your personal vow of surrender and commitment to God—your vow to Him for today, tomorrow, and the rest of your life.

    _____

    _____

    _____

DH Field Notes:

_____

_____

_____

09. Finishing Well

Mike recounts the moving story of his first wife's personal battle with, and ultimate defeat by, Hodgkin's disease. Her inspiring example provides him with memorable insights into what makes life precious, and how even "unacceptable risk" and certain death can be redeemed for life when God is allowed to reign over the details. Mike ends his conversation with a compelling definition of epiphany—a spiritual awakening that catches us by surprise and changes our life forever. But an epiphany is a gift of God, not something we can engineer. So Mike's closing challenge is to do the one thing that radicals least want to do—quit. Because when we quit in surrender to God, He can accomplish in us and through what He's been waiting to do all along.

1. How did you respond to Lisa's story? Do you know others who have finished their lives well under extremely trying circumstances? What did observing their examples teach you?

   _____

   _____

   _____

2. Is there a Bible promise that your life will end up the way you want? What does the Bible say about how followers of Christ should finish their lives? (See Philippians 1–3; 2 Timothy; Hebrews 10:19–13:21.)

   _____

   _____

   _____

3. Mike asks the question, "How can I get more out of my death?" How would you answer that question for yourself?

   _____

   _____

   _____

4. Have you ever experienced an epiphany—or moment of powerful spiritual enlightenment? Describe it here and for your small group, and how it has affected your life.

   _____

   _____

   _____

5. Did you pray the prayer at the end of the book? Write
   down what you prayed here so that it can become an
   even stronger part of your consciousness. Write out or
   talk about what this prayer means to you now, and
   what you hope it will mean to you in the days ahead.

   _____

   _____

   _____

DH Field Notes:

_____

_____

_____